CELEBR
CHRISTIAN

The Alcuin Liturgy Guides (ALG) revive the tradition of the Alcuin Manual, and address both practical and theoretical questions concerning the practice of worship, its setting and celebration.

The first two Alcuin Liturgy Guides, *Memorial Services* by Donald Gray, and *Art and Worship* by Anne Dawtry and Christopher Irvine, were published by SPCK in 2002. ALG 3, *Celebrating the Eucharist*, by Benjamin Gordon-Taylor and Simon Jones, was published in 2005 (reissued 2011), and ALG 4, *The Use of Symbols in Worship*, edited by Christopher Irvine, was published in 2007. Two further volumes on the celebration of the liturgical year followed: *Celebrating Christ's Appearing* (ALG 5) in 2008, and *Celebrating Christ's Victory* (ALG 6) in 2009. The series now continues with the present volume.

Members of the Alcuin Club receive free copies of the annual Collection, the Liturgy Guides and the Joint Liturgical Studies. Founded in 1897, the Alcuin Club seeks to promote the study of Christian liturgy in general, with special reference to worship in the Anglican Communion in particular. The chairman of the Alcuin Club is the Revd Canon Christopher Irvine, the Secretary is the Revd Dr Gordon Jeanes, and details regarding membership, the annual subscription and lists of publications can be obtained from the Club's office: The Alcuin Club, 5 Saffron Street, Royston, Hertfordshire SG8 9TR.

Visit the Alcuin Club website at **www.alcuinclub.org.uk**

CELEBRATING CHRISTIAN INITIATION

*Baptism, confirmation and
rites for the Christian journey*

SIMON JONES

Alcuin Liturgy Guides 7

First published in Great Britain in 2016

Society for Promoting Christian Knowledge
36 Causton Street
London SW1P 4ST
www.spck.org.uk

British Library Cataloguing-in-Publication Data
A catalogue record for this book is available from the British Library

ISBN 978–0–281–07537–9
eBook ISBN 978–0–281–07538–6

Typeset by Graphicraft Limited, Hong Kong
First printed in Great Britain by Ashford Colour Press
Subsequently digitally printed in Great Britain

eBook by Graphicraft Limited, Hong Kong

Produced on paper from sustainable forests

Contents

Preface		vii
Abbreviations		viii
Introduction		ix
1	Drama, setting and symbol	1
2	Rites on the Way: infants and children	14
3	Rites on the Way: adults	27
4	The baptism of infants and children	42
5	The baptism and confirmation of adults	77
6	Rites of affirmation and reception	103
	Sources and further reading	118
	Index	121

Contents

Preface

This volume is dedicated to those at Tewkesbury Abbey and Merton College whom I have helped to prepare for, and with whom I have been privileged to celebrate, the sacraments of Christian initiation. I am grateful for the way in which they have contributed to my understanding of these rites as well as helping me to reflect on how they should be performed. I am also indebted to the Revd Dr Benjamin Gordon-Taylor, Editorial Secretary of the Alcuin Club and to Philip Law at SPCK. Above all, thanks are due to my colleagues at Merton for granting me sabbatical leave to work on this project, to the Revd Canon Dr Paul Bradshaw and Merton colleagues for taking over the reins of the chaplaincy during my absence, and to the brothers of the Society of St John the Evangelist in Cambridge, Massachusetts, for welcoming me into their community and providing an hospitable and stimulating environment in which to worship and work.

S.M.J.

Abbreviations

ALG 3	Benjamin Gordon-Taylor and Simon Jones, *Celebrating the Eucharist*, Alcuin Liturgy Guides 3.
ALG 4	Christopher Irvine (ed.), *The Use of Symbols in Worship*, Alcuin Liturgy Guides 4.
ALG 5	Benjamin Gordon-Taylor and Simon Jones, *Celebrating Christ's Appearing*, Alcuin Liturgy Guides 5.
ALG 6	Benjamin Gordon-Taylor and Simon Jones, *Celebrating Christ's Victory*, Alcuin Liturgy Guides 6.
ASB	*The Alternative Service Book 1980.*
ATAL	*Common Worship: Christian Initiation: Additional Baptism Texts in Accessible Language.*
BACSI	Baptism as Complete Sacramental Initiation (see 1991 report of the International Anglican Liturgical Consultation (IALC), Known as the Toronto Statement).
BCP 1662	The Book of Common Prayer 1662.
BCP 1979	The Book of Common Prayer 1979 (USA).
BOS	*The Book of Occasional Services 2003* (USA).
CCW1	Paul Bradshaw, *A Companion to Common Worship* Vol. 1.
CCW2	Paul Bradshaw, *A Companion to Common Worship* Vol. 2.
CI	*Common Worship: Christian Initiation.*
CW	Common Worship.
CWMV	*Common Worship: Services and Prayers for the Church of England* (Common Worship 'Main Volume').
DP	*Common Worship: Daily Prayer.*
NPFW	*New Patterns for Worship.*
OS	*Common Worship: Ordination Services.*
PMC	*Common Worship: A Pastoral Ministry Companion.*
PS	*Common Worship: Pastoral Services.*
RCIA	*Rite of Christian Initiation of Adults.*
TS	*Common Worship: Times and Seasons.*

Introduction

Leading people in worship is leading people into mystery, into the unknown and yet the familiar; this spiritual activity is much more than getting the words or the sections in the right order. The primary object in the careful planning and leading of the service is the spiritual direction which enables the whole congregation to come into the presence of God to give him glory, and then to go out energized for mission.

(CI: p. 329)

In our introduction to *Celebrating the Eucharist*, Benjamin Gordon-Taylor and I noted that it was the latest among a 'surprising number of manuals of Anglican origin and authorship which have sought to encourage sound practice in the celebration of the Eucharist in the Church of England and the Anglican Communion more generally' (ALG 3: p. xi). At the time, the same could not be said about equivalent guides to the celebration of Christian initiation and, ten years later, with few exceptions (see pp. 118–20), the situation has changed very little.

Why is this? Is it that initiation rites are much simpler to celebrate than the Eucharist, and so require less guidance? (Dearmer, in *The Parson's Handbook* (1932), devoted just 28 pages to baptism, catechism and confirmation out of a total of almost 500; more recently, in Michno's *A Priest's Handbook* (1998) they account for 11 out of 300.) Or is it that, compared with the Eucharist, there is much less diversity in belief and practice, removing the need for manuals which encourage a certain style of celebration to express a particular theological stance? Or even that, since deacons and, *in extremis*, lay people may baptize, it is perceived as being less central to priestly and episcopal ministry. While all of these may, to an extent, be true, perhaps the most likely explanation is that baptism is viewed as mattering less than the Eucharist, or being less significant, both to individual Christians and the wider Church, so that, consequently, the manner of its celebration has received less attention. Pointing a finger at myself, this is especially true of Anglican Catholics. Compare the amount of time typically devoted to preparing for a 'first Mass' compared to a 'first baptism'!

My contention is that the celebration of Christian initiation is as much a 'leading people into mystery', the mystery of God, as is the celebration of the Eucharist, and therefore requires as much attention. Thus this volume endeavours to provide a detailed manual for the celebration of Christian initiation. Faithful to the ethos of the Alcuin Club, it does so within a broadly Catholic tradition, with the hope that its contents will also be of use to those who belong elsewhere. It focuses on *Common Worship: Christian Initiation*, published in 2006, in a way that means many of the principles of performance may be applied to other initiation rites within Anglicanism and beyond. Following other Alcuin Liturgy Guides, its advice arises from an engagement with liturgical history and theology while, at the same time, being rooted in the pastoral reality of the variety of settings in which the Church finds herself ministering. In this connection, it draws on insights from, and makes reference to, the Church of England's adult discipleship course, 'Pilgrim', as well as the work of the Archbishops' Council Baptism Research and Resources group (hereafter 'the Baptism Project').

The changing face of Christian initiation: baptismal identity, catechumenate, confirmation

The fact that so little has been written about the performance of initiation rites is surprising given that twentieth-century liturgical scholarship and renewal have left their marks on the theology and rites of Christian initiation no less than the Eucharist. In the Church of England, scholarly contributions from a number of liturgists (among them, in the middle of the last century, Gregory Dix and Geoffrey Lampe) drew implications for contemporary practice from research into what could be known about the early history and development of initiation. As far back as 1968, the Lambeth Conference asked each province of the Anglican Communion to explore the relationship between baptism and confirmation. A similar request was made, ecumenically, by the World Council of Churches in its Lima Statement (*Baptism, Eucharist, Ministry*, 1982), challenging all churches to re-examine their theology and practice of initiation.

Within Anglicanism, provinces have revised their initiation services at different speeds and in slightly different directions. It is not the purpose of this guide to trace these developments. As far as the Church

of England is concerned, the debate has often centred on the relationship between baptism, confirmation and the Eucharist. Indeed, it
could be argued that the identity crisis surrounding confirmation
has been one of the principal catalysts for the renewal of baptismal
theology. That said, the confirmation conundrum is just one area to
be considered in any exploration of the changing face of Christian
initiation. As significant are what might be broadly termed 'baptismal
identity' as well as the revival of the catechumenate. Given that these
receive thorough treatment in the introduction to CI (CI: pp. 3–12)
and the Liturgical Commission's commentary (CI: pp. 314–50), both
of which are essential reading for those who preside at rites of
Christian initiation, they will be touched on briefly here, allowing
the more complex issue of the relationship between baptism, confirmation and Eucharist to have more thorough treatment.

Baptismal identity

Baptism is not only the centre point around which the other rites
in CI are clustered. It also provides the theological underpinning
for a number of other rites within the family of CW, with the result
that it is presented as fundamental to the Church's identity and
mission. Although the Church of England has not elevated 'baptismal
ecclesiology' to the status it enjoys in The Episcopal Church (see Myers
1997), its presence can, nevertheless, be felt, not least in rites of recon-
ciliation, healing and wholeness (CI: pp. 351–4) and ordination (OS:
pp. 10, 32, 55, 124), as well as the initiation services themselves.

All of this draws attention away from seeing baptism as an iso-
lated ritual moment, disconnected from Christian life and witness;
rather, as described by the 1995 report, *On the Way*, it is viewed as a
'sacrament of significance in its own right that points Christians to their
true identity, character and calling' (*On the Way*: p. 62). The work
of members of the Liturgical Commission, Board of Education and
Board of Mission, and many of the recommendations found in *On the
Way*, as well as its overall theology, find expression in CI, and several
of the key sections from the report have been included in the commentary (CI: p. 314). Its influence cannot be exaggerated, and leads
CI to describe baptism as:

> much more than a beginning to the Christian life. It expresses the
> identity which is ours in Jesus Christ and the shape of the life to which

we are called ... Baptism is a reality whose meaning has to be discovered at each stage of a person's life ... One test of the liturgical celebration of baptism is whether, over time, it enables the whole Church to see itself as a baptized community, called to partake in the life of God and to share in the mission of God to the world.   (CI: p. 10)

The challenge for those who prepare candidates for, and celebrate, rites of Christian initiation is how to do this in such a way that expresses 'the identity and call of the Christian community today' (CI: p. 3). This is a point which will be returned to on a number of occasions in this and subsequent chapters, approaching it from various perspectives. For further discussion, in addition to the Liturgical Commission's commentary, see also Haselock (2000).

Catechumenate

The number of adults being baptized in the Church of England has increased substantially in recent years. From 2004 to 2013, whereas infant baptism declined by 17 per cent, the baptism of children (from 5 to 12 years of age) grew by 15 per cent, and adult baptism increased by 32 per cent from 8,000 to 11,000 per annum (Research and Statistics Department of the Archbishops' Council, *Statistics for Mission 2013*). This significant growth has coincided with baptism being seen as 'the culmination of an accompanied journey of exploration and enquiry (the catechumenate model)' (CI: p. 5) within a process of Christian initiation. That the catechumenate should be seen as 'a useful model against which to review and improve initiation practice in the Church of England' was one of the major recommendations of *On the Way* (1995: p. 48). In CW, the stages of this journey are marked by a number of liturgical rites which, like the Roman Catholic *Rite of Christian Initiation of Adults*, are inspired by the catechumenate of the early centuries of the Christian Church. It is striking that, ten years after they were first published, very few communities seem to make use of the catechumenal material published in CI. Since this is a relatively new development for the Church of England, with no equivalent rites in ASB or BCP 1662, clergy and lay leaders may not be aware that the material exists, or be uncertain of how to make best use of it, or be overwhelmed by the amount of material provided.

It is to be hoped that this is now changing, and that the wide-spread use of the Church of England's adult discipleship course, Pilgrim (<www.pilgrimcourse.org>), will encourage fresh interest in a catechumenal approach to initiation. Pilgrim is 'a course for the Christian journey' whose aim is 'to help people become disciples of Jesus Christ' (Croft 2013, *Pilgrim: Leader's Guide*: p. 10). Its advent provides an opportunity for Christian communities to think afresh about how worship and catechesis can form new Christians, and renew and strengthen those already baptized. This is not to say that other discipleship courses may not be used with the Church of England's catechumenal rites; far from it. What is important is that catechumenal rites are not used without catechesis and vice versa.

Confirmation

It is no exaggeration to say that, in the last 150 years, most discussion of Christian initiation, particularly among Anglicans, has either been hijacked by, or run aground because of, arguments over the history and purpose of confirmation. At its heart lies a dispute about what can be said to constitute 'complete sacramental initiation'.

On the one side there are those who believe that baptism *and* confirmation are both rites of initiation which are necessary for participation in the Eucharist. Often referred to as the Mason–Dix line (after Arthur Mason and Gregory Dix who were two of its most influential proponents), in this view confirmation is an essential part of Christian initiation, conferring the seal of the Spirit and completing baptism.

The opposite view is most commonly referred to as BACSI: Baptism as Complete Sacramental Initiation, a theology which finds its most concise articulation in the 1991 report of the International Anglican Liturgical Consultation (IALC), known as the Toronto Statement. Its third recommendation states 'baptism is complete sacramental initiation and leads to participation in the Eucharist' (Holeton 1993: p. 229).

Where does the Church of England stand with respect to these two positions? Three relatively recent developments seemed to ring the death knell for Mason–Dix: the admission of baptized children to communion before confirmation, the publication of *On the Way* (1995) and the authorization of the CW rites of baptism and confirmation (1998).

Communion before confirmation is now the normal pattern of initiation in a significant number of parishes. Permitted experimentally in three dioceses as far back as 1974, the decision to admit children rests with individual parishes which apply to the bishop for permission.

Relating to Canon B15A, the 2006 regulations are published with the *Canons of the Church of England* (<www.churchofengland.org/about-us/structure/churchlawlegis/canons/canons-7th-edition.aspx>). Since these regulations have opened up a direct route from infant baptism to first communion it is no longer possible for the Church of England to say that it regards confirmation as an *essential* part of the initiatory process. The Pastoral Introduction to the rite of admission states that 'A person is admitted to communion on the basis of their baptism' (CI: p. 189).

What then of confirmation? *On the Way* saw 'great merit' in the suggestion of David Stancliffe and Kenneth Stevenson that there could be 'a renewed and extended view of Confirmation, akin to the Pastoral Offices, in which the bishop's role is the norm' (*On the Way*: p. 68). This echoed the second half of the BACSI recommendation of the Toronto Statement:

> Confirmation and other rites of affirmation have a continuing pastoral role in the renewal of faith among the baptized but are in no way to be seen as a completion of baptism or as necessary for admission to communion. (Holeton 1993: p. 229)

So does the Church of England now view confirmation as a pastoral rather than initiatory rite? Yes and no! The 'extended view of confirmation' can certainly be found in CW, not least in the provision of an almost identical rite of Affirmation of Baptismal Faith for those already baptized and confirmed who wish to make a public commitment of faith. This includes the laying on of hands, optional anointing, and a version of the classic BCP 1662 confirmation prayer, 'Defend, O Lord'. Furthermore, when baptism and confirmation are combined, the separate identities of the two rites are hardly visible. Within one integrated celebration of Christian initiation it requires no stretch of the liturgical imagination to interpret the prayer, laying on of hands and optional anointing of confirmation as post-baptismal ceremonies, rather than a rite within a rite. This is particularly true if confirmation takes place at the font, and if there are no confirmands who have already been baptized at the same service.

However, just when it looked like the Church of England might be putting the first nails in the Mason–Dix coffin, an opposing view made an unexpected appearance. A report of the Faith and Order Commission of the Church of England, *The Journey of Christian*

Initiation (Avis 2011), offered a rationale for confirmation which put clear water between itself and BACSI:

> This report affirms the integrity of confirmation as an outward and visible sign of an inward and spiritual grace and its vital place in the overall process of Christian initiation . . . Baptism stands at the heart of Christian initiation, but it is not all there is to initiation. Confirmation is an important further step, a subsequent gift, and initiation is not complete until we have made our first communion. (Avis 2011: p. 4)

The result of all this is a Church of England which is, to say the least, confused about the relationship between baptism and confirmation. Where does this guide position itself in this debate? For theological, liturgical and pastoral reasons, BACSI underpins the chapters of this volume, but not uncritically so. According to the Toronto Statement, 'Full membership of the Church is conferred through baptism' (Holeton 1993: p. 243). But what about the Eucharist? Whatever view one might take about a post-baptismal rite of confirmation, is it possible to talk about full membership of the Church without reference to being fed at the table of the Lord? Perhaps the minds of early proponents of BACSI were so focused on removing confirmation from the initiatory process that they underestimated the significance of the Eucharist as a sacrament of initiation in its own right, not simply in terms of it being the rite to which baptism leads, but also to it being the repeatable part of the initiatory process. Twenty years after Toronto, a 2011 study document of the World Council of Churches stated:

> The one unrepeatable baptism leads a Christian to the regular, repeated participation in the Lord's supper. The Eucharistic meal marks the culmination of Christian initiation . . . Theologically and liturgically, membership appears to be 'incomplete' prior to admission to the Eucharist. (*One Baptism* 2011: § 60, 64)

This may highlight a lacuna in the Toronto Statement, but it does not weaken the main thrust of what it has to say about the relationship between baptism and confirmation. With this in mind, the strong recommendation of this guide is that adults should be baptized, confirmed and make their first communion within a single episcopal rite. Although this will not always be possible, there is a serious danger of undermining the significance of baptism if it is separated from the rites of confirmation and Eucharist. If there are strong reasons to separate baptism and confirmation, baptism should be celebrated at a principal service on a Sunday or festival within the context of the Eucharist, at which the newly baptized make their first communion. Although the commentary rightly points out that the discipline of the Church of England permits two liturgical sequences when adults are baptized, to be admitted to communion after baptism *or* after confirmation (CI: p. 338), to wait until the candidate has been confirmed implies a two-stage Mason–Dix theology: that, after baptism, their membership of the Body of Christ is incomplete and that confirmation bestows an additional grace, the reception of which is necessary before receiving communion. Since the Church of England permits baptized children to receive communion before confirmation, this makes no sense. For a detailed critique of *The Journey of Christian Initiation* and a robust defence of BACSI, see Buchanan (2014).

In summary, CW has not solved the confirmation conundrum; that was never its intention. If anything, the situation is more confused now than it has ever been (see Jones 1995: p. 288). A variety of practices, some of them conflicting, exist within the Church of England and CI seeks to accommodate them. It is therefore the responsibility of each Christian community to work out where it stands within this spectrum of belief and practice and, from this starting point, make appropriate use of the liturgical material provided.

The baptism of infants and the Baptism Project

The baptism of infants provides its own challenges and opportunities which are well known to clergy and ministry teams. After the success of the Weddings Project, the Church of England turned its attention to the baptism of infants in its Baptism Project. Its greatest strength is that it is informed by research 'to help find out why families choose to have their children baptized, and why they might choose not to' (<https://churchsupporthub.org/baptisms/explore-thinking>). This provides a helpful insight into people's experience of the baptism rite as well as any preparation or follow-up. The available material includes:

- <https://churchofenglandchristenings.org/> – a website providing 'all you need to know about choosing, planning and going to a Church of England christening';

- <https://churchsupporthub.org/baptisms/> – a website providing resources and ideas for clergy and others involved in baptism ministry;
- <https://www.churchprinthub.org/> – a website from which a range of attractively produced printed materials can be bought, including christening cards for parents and godparents, follow-up invitations and prayer postcards.

One of the most fundamental differences between CW and both BCP 1662 and ASB is that CW provides one baptismal rite for use with candidates of any age. This has significant implications for the celebration of Christian initiation. Advocated by the first International Anglican Liturgical Consultation in Boston in 1985 (Holeton 1993: p. 254), this guide strongly supports the theological principle of one baptism for all. It upholds the important theological principle that there is 'one Lord, one faith, one baptism' (Ephesians 4.5) and that, as a result, great care should be taken to ensure that the baptism of infants is not performed in a way that suggests that it is somehow inferior to that of adults. That said, for pastoral and practical reasons, not least that adults and infants will often be baptized separately, and that the preparation of adult candidates is likely to differ considerably from that for parents and godparents, this guide will give separate consideration to the celebration of initiation rites for adults (Chapters 3 and 5) and infants (Chapters 2 and 4), with further notes detailing how to celebrate a rite in which both infants and adults are being baptized (pp. 96–7).

Whatever the age of the candidates, the canonical expectation is that baptism should be celebrated 'when the most number of people come together' (Canon B21). Moreover, in the case of infants, Baptism Project research suggests that there are significant missional advantages in doing so, with 29 per cent of parents being likely to become regular church members compared with 14 per cent when baptism is celebrated as a stand-alone rite.

Nevertheless, the same research reveals that around 60 per cent of infant baptisms still take place apart from public worship. The pastoral reasons given for justifying this practice are well known: among them, that Sunday morning is an inconvenient time for parents who need to get children ready and guests travelling some distance; that, in some parishes, the number of requests for infant baptism would mean that they would take over the Sunday morning service at least once a month; if the service is eucharistic, it can exclude a significant proportion of the congregation; and, not least, that visitors often outnumber regular members of the congregation on 'baptism Sundays', with the result that some of the regulars stay away, or go to another service. While not wanting to condone this practice, these problems are real, and there remains a need to give guidance on how best to use the CW provision for baptism when it has to be celebrated as a stand-alone service, often in the late morning or early afternoon on a Sunday, with very few, if any, members of the congregation present (pp. 46–66). Those wishing to move away from stand-alone rites to celebrate baptisms within the principal Sunday service will find some useful advice on how this might be achieved at <https://churchsupporthub.org/baptisms/>.

The 'one-size-fits-all' approach of CW relates not only to the age of candidates for baptism, but also to the variety of contexts in which the Church finds herself ministering. This variety requires a degree of flexibility within the rite to meet the needs of different groups of people in different contexts. It is therefore not surprising that, since it was first authorized in 1998, two pieces of synodical business have been introduced to revise, albeit in a limited way, the CW service of Holy Baptism which, notably, was the only principal CW rite not to have been road-tested through experimental use. Unsurprising, too, is that both relate primarily to its use with infants. Responding to early criticism about the length of the rite and the number of mandatory elements, the General Synod, through its *Miscellaneous Liturgical Proposals* (GS 1342, 1999), allowed for greater flexibility than was originally permitted. The rite published in CWMV and CI incorporates these. Subsequently, in 2011, in response to a motion from the Diocese of Liverpool, the House of Bishops asked the Liturgical Commission to prepare supplementary material aimed at those who are unused to attending church, and who found the existing CW provision complex and inaccessible. After the initiation services were first published, Jeremy Haselock rightly pointed out:

> The new *Common Worship* baptism service draws upon the enormous variety of imagery used in the New Testament to illustrate the richness of all that God gives us through the sacrament.
>
> (Haselock 2000: pp. 1–2)

But at what cost? This was one of the new rite's great strengths, but also its principal weakness. Specifically, therefore, the Liturgical Commission was asked to provide alternative texts for the Decision, the Prayer over the Water, and the Commission, as well as any other elements of the rite which were thought to require revision. This led to the authorization of *Christian Initiation: Additional Baptism Texts in Accessible Language* (hereafter ATAL) from 1 September 2015.

The experience of using the rite over more than 15 years will have suggested to some that it might have been better to revisit some of the first principles upon which the initiation rites were devised, and start afresh, rather than attempting to manipulate the existing provision into an accessible form by substituting a few new words. That road not having been taken, greater flexibility than is often recognized and a selection of new texts nevertheless provide an opportune moment for clergy and parishes to think again about how they celebrate Christian initiation, not only in terms of texts used, but also in the manner in which they are performed. This is particularly true of celebrations of infant baptism. Interestingly, Baptism Project research revealed very little negative comment about the CW texts, perhaps suggesting that anxiety about their use was more an issue for clergy than congregations. While welcoming ATAL, it is important to remember that changing a few words, even important ones, will not enable people to engage with what is going on, and participate in a new way, without also considering how they are performed. Liturgical texts are always more than words on a page; they are prayed text-in-performance, and need to be approached as such (see pp. 1–2 and ALG 3: pp. xvii–xviii).

As yet, no reference has been made to the most important preparations for infant baptism: that of the child's parents and godparents and, indeed, of the congregation itself, so that they may be 'put in remembrance of their own profession made to God at their baptism' (Canon B21). This falls outside the remit of a liturgical guide, but there are many excellent resources available. See also Ron Dowling, 'Preparing Parents for Infant Baptism' (Holeton 1993: pp. 94–102). The message of this volume is that however meticulously planned and expertly performed the liturgy is, it will never make redundant the need for proper preparation and appropriate follow-up to assist in 'leading people into mystery'.

1

Drama, setting and symbol

The drama of Christian initiation

To celebrate rites of Christian initiation is to participate in the drama of salvation. The fourth-century Bishop of Jerusalem, St Cyril, explains this fundamental truth to those who had recently undergone the 'awe-inspiring rites of initiation':

> What a strange and astonishing situation! We did not really die, we were not really buried, we did not really hang from a cross and rise again. Our imitation was symbolic, but our salvation a reality.
>
> (*Mystagogical Catechesis* 2.5; Yarnold 1994: p. 78)

Cyril's understanding of baptism is influenced by the initiation rites of Greek and Roman mystery-religions. As Edward Yarnold explains:

> the candidate witnessed a representation of episodes in the life of a god or goddess, and himself took part in the action ... The typological link ... between the initiate and the god which the rites were designed to create was not simply an internal spiritual effect. The intention was to allow the drama of the rite to produce an intense and lasting psychological experience of conversion and happiness. As Aristotle understood the mysteries, 'those undergoing initiation are not expected to gain knowledge (*mathein*) but an experience (*pathein*) and a disposition' (Aristotle, frag. 45, 1483a19).   (Yarnold 1982: p. 26)

One of the purposes of this guide is to encourage clergy and catechists to raise the spiritual expectations of those preparing for initiation to such a level, and to celebrate the sacraments of initiation in such a way, that those who experience them are able to testify to an intense and life-transforming encounter with Christ crucified and risen through the anointing of the Holy Spirit.

For many this may seem like an unachievable aim, but one step towards making it a reality is to recover confidence in liturgy, a lack of which impoverishes many contemporary Christian communities. In general terms, there is a temptation to disbelieve that liturgical worship 'does what it says on the tin'. This lack of trust can manifest itself in various ways; chief among them, the temptation to turn worship into entertainment, and the need to explain everything that is about to happen before it takes place. Both of these are often motivated by the desire to make services more mission-oriented, helping people to feel welcome and included. But there are other ways of doing that.

There is another emerging orthodoxy, possibly, in part, a reaction to the crisis of confidence, which can also undermine the liturgy. This is a sort of inward-looking rubricism, which sees doing what it says as of paramount importance, and the role of ritual in enabling active participation as, at best, secondary. Those who are influenced by this way of thinking may be tempted to hurry through the liturgy, believing that all that matters is *that*, rather than *how*, the prescribed words are said. In terms of ritual, a minimal *orans* position, with the hands a few inches apart, fulfils the rubrics and is therefore sufficient, whether it can be seen by the congregation or not.

Challenging both of these trends, Cyril of Jerusalem encourages the contemporary Church to perform rites of Christian initiation as drama. In a liturgical performance, there are no passive spectators, but every member of the worshipping community, ordained and lay, is an active participant with a role to play. If this is true, then the way in which the liturgy is staged and performed can have negative as well as positive results, as James Turrell explains:

> The performance of the liturgy can assist in bringing out its meaning and in facilitating the participation of the assembly; it can undercut the theology of the rite and short-circuit the meaningful participation of the faithful; or it can simply desiccate the rite, sucking the life out of it. Baptism and the rites of confirmation/reception/reaffirmation must be carefully prepared and performed, or we can inadvertently undermine the liturgy. (Turrell 2013: p. 70)

Addressing the challenge to breathe life back into rites of initiation or, rather, to allow the Holy Spirit to do so, is one of the tasks of this volume.

The setting of Christian initiation

Understanding the celebration of Christian initiation as dramatic performance requires attention to be paid to its setting. The importance of place, the way it is used and the arrangement of furniture within it, is now commonly discussed in relation to the Eucharist (see ALG 3: ch. 2). Less attention is paid to it with respect to the celebration of initiation. The reordering of churches will often focus on the east end, in particular the position and design of the altar-table, without making the necessary connection between font and altar, and that what happens at one has implications for the other.

ALG 3 commented on many of the principal liturgical furnishings used in celebrating the Eucharist (ALG 3: pp. 8–12). This guide will look at them again, together with those associated with Christian initiation. The principles governing the way in which initiation rites are staged are no different from those relating to the Eucharist. Indeed, the use of font and Easter Candle needs to be considered as part of the stage-setting of the Eucharist, even when initiation is celebrated as a non-eucharistic rite. In text and in ritual, a connection needs to be made between font and altar since, within the rites of Christian initiation, theologically, liturgically and ecclesiologically, baptism and Eucharist belong together.

The font

1 In every church and chapel where baptism is to be administered, there shall be provided a decent font with a cover for the keeping clean thereof.
2 The font shall stand as near to the principal entrance as conveniently may be, except there by a custom to the contrary or the Ordinary otherwise direct; and shall be set in as spacious and well-ordered surroundings as possible.
3 The font bowl shall only be used for the water at the administration of Holy Baptism and for no other purpose whatsoever.

(*Canons of the Church of England*, F1 – Of the font)

Given the encouragement of the canons to site the font in 'as spacious and well-ordered surroundings as possible', it is surprising how many fonts find themselves in inaccessible corners, surrounded by pews, hemmed in by hymn book trolleys, obscured by a crib at Christmas, or home to a display of garden produce at harvest! Sometimes, without major reordering, there's very little that can be done about how accessible a font is. However, de-cluttering a space is often a possibility. In churches where pieces of furniture have been placed round the font, and its lid is used as a surface on which to put the parish magazine, the impression given, often unintentionally, is that the font or, to be more precise, baptism, is of little significance. Whereas, if the place of baptism is thought to be important, not only for those who come to be washed in it, but also for the whole community, reminding them that through its waters they have become members of 'a chosen race, a royal priesthood, a holy nation, God's own people' (1 Peter 2.9a), then, as Richard Giles suggests, the aim must be for it to be 'a place of permanent significance clearly demarcated from the rest of the area of liturgical assembly' (Giles 1997: p. 167).

Giles is uncompromising when he suggests that, if the place of baptism can't be a space around which people can gather, not only for celebrations of initiation, but also at the beginning of the Eucharist and at other times, a radical solution is required:

> In many church buildings, to gather round the existing font is almost a practical impossibility, but do it nevertheless. Do it when only a few can get within touching distance, do it with people standing on pews or sitting on window sills. Do it until the cry goes up, 'How long, O Lord, how long . . . before we can build a proper font?'
>
> (Giles 2004: p. 102)

As to what a 'proper font' might look like, Regina Kuehn suggests that it has a twofold purpose: 'First, it *reveals* by its shape part of the truth about baptism. Second, the font *points* to the water' (Kuehn 1992: p. viii).

If building a 'proper font' is not an option, then to make the best of what is given is nearly always better than using a portable font or a bowl on a table. For Giles, a portable font demeans baptism (Giles 2004: p. 102). For Aidan Kavanagh, 'Altars on wheels, fonts that collapse, and presidential chairs that fold away do not free but neuter liturgical space' (Kavanagh 1982: p. 17). In my view, it is not so much that a portable font belittles the sacrament (though it clearly falls short of the canonical expectation) or neutralizes the space it is in as that, if the font is only wheeled out when it is required, it fails to fulfil its purpose of reminding the Christian community of its baptismal calling and identity every time they gather for worship. Another disadvantage is that, if positioned somewhere at the east end, it will often compete with the altar for centre-stage and, without its own space and setting, lose out. To quote Kavanagh again:

4

Neither altar nor font should be so close to the other as to compete for attention or to confuse each other's purpose, dignity, and quite different kinds of liturgy. The altar is a table to dine upon. The font is a pool to bathe in, a womb to be born from, a tomb to be buried in. Bathing and dining areas are rarely found in the same room, except in churches.   (Kavanagh 1982: p. 17)

How can the font be used as a sign of baptismal vocation? Giles advocates the people journeying to the font at the beginning of the Eucharist for the Prayers of Penitence, and being sprinkled with its waters. If there is space for people to gather round the font, there are times in the Christian year when this would be particularly appropriate (see, for example, a suggested rite for Advent in ALG 3: pp. 36–7). If there is not enough space, the congregation can at least be encouraged to turn towards the font for the opening rite.

At funerals, if it is customary to sprinkle the coffin when it is brought into church (see PS: p. 295), it may be possible for the coffin to be brought to the font so that it can be sprinkled from there, proclaiming in a vivid symbolic gesture that baptismal identity is not destroyed by death, and that if, in the waters of the font, 'we have been united with him in a death like his, we will certainly be united with him in a resurrection like his' (Romans 6.5).

The canons refer to the font having a cover, but Giles is very much against them: 'take off (and lose) its lid', Giles advises, 'and fill it with water until it overflows' (Giles 2004: p. 102). Indeed, a number of fonts installed in recent decades have been designed in such a way that they are open and accessible to worshippers and visitors alike, containing a generous amount of water; for example, Portsmouth and Salisbury Cathedrals, the Church of the Community of the Resurrection at Mirfield, and Giles' own former parish, St Thomas' Church, Huddersfield. Without a cover, the font becomes a permanent rather than temporary place of baptismal significance, and may be used as a stoup, reminding those arriving for worship of their baptismal identity, particularly if they are encouraged to use its water to sign themselves with the cross.

Such a practice may be against the letter of paragraph three of Canon F1, but the CW rites of confirmation, affirmation and reception all permit candidates to 'come forward to the font and sign themselves with water, or the president may sprinkle them' (CI: pp. 117, 203, 217), whether or not baptism is celebrated at the same service, and this is surely to be encouraged. It is also another reason to try to make the area round the font as spacious as possible.

If the font is designed for baptism by immersion, it should be used for infants as well as adults. Although it may be tempting not to, if the font is used for adults and a portable font or bowl for infants, the impression given is that infant baptism is, in some way, inferior or second class. Whether infants are baptized by immersion or not, the same font should normally be used for all candidates for baptism.

Finally, if the font is not suitable for immersion, but that is the desired method of baptizing, it may be possible to borrow a baptismal pool, hire a birthing pool, ask a nearby church which has a baptismal pool if the service could take place there, or go to a river or beach.

The Easter Candle

Not more than a few decades ago, an Easter (or Paschal) Candle would only be seen in churches of a definite Anglo-Catholic tradition. Nowadays its use is relatively widespread and, even if it is not marked, lit from a fire and carried in procession at the Easter Vigil (for commentary on Easter Vigil in TS, see ALG 6: pp. 67–86); and it will often be lit at baptisms so that the candidates' candles can be lit from it. Unlike the font and a number of other ecclesiastical fixtures and fittings, the absence of any reference to the Easter Candle in the canons suggests that it has no official standing or significance in the Church of England, and this is reflected in CI referring to it, somewhat coyly, as a 'large candle' (see, for example, CI: p. 67). That said, large is what it should definitely be, normally the largest candle in the church, a new one each year, not last year's recycled (Elliott 2002: p. 130), decorated and marked (TS: pp. 408–9), sometimes with a ring of flowers around the base, and placed in its own stand. The latter, according to Giles, 'needs to be substantial and robust, not flimsy, or inconsequential, or easily knocked over' (Giles 2008: p. 143).

The association of the Easter Candle with baptism is an important one. Although liturgical scholars no longer identify Easter as the only time when early Christian communities celebrated the rites of initiation (see, for example, Bradshaw and Johnson 2011: pp. 75–86), the Easter Vigil is, nevertheless, the liturgy of initiation par excellence. As the principal symbolic focus of the risen Christ, the light of Easter not only pierces the darkness of sin with hope and new life, but is also used in the blessing of the font. The candle is plunged into the water once or three times, symbolizing the way in which the water becomes the means by which candidates for baptism participate in the paschal mystery.

Although the Easter Candle is traditionally placed near the altar or ambo in Eastertide, by the font at other times in the year, and next to the coffin at funerals, the size and layout of the liturgical space will often suggest where best to locate its stand. At the font, it needs to be in a prominent position so that it is visible to the congregation during baptism, without preventing people from gathering round the font; if the candidates' candles are to be lit from it, it needs to be accessible enough to make this possible. In the sanctuary it may either stand next to the ambo, illuminating the proclamation of God's word, or on the north side of the altar. Its position should not obscure altar or ambo, but it should be clearly associated with one or other, rather than being detached and standing independently. If placed near the altar, when incense is used at the Eucharist, the Easter Candle may be censed in place of the cross or crucifix during the censing of the altar at the entrance rite and offertory (see ALG 3: p. 31). At the Easter Liturgy, and at other services on Easter Day, it may be placed at the centre of the sanctuary (see Elliott 2002, p. 131), although, preferably, not so as to distract people's attention from the celebration of the liturgy itself. (For a more detailed description of how light symbolizes enlightenment within rites of Christian initiation, see ALG 4: pp. 73–8.)

The ambo or lectern

Whether or not initiation takes place within the context of the Eucharist, it is important for there to be a focal point for the proclamation of God's word. Christian initiation is no less a celebration of word and sacrament than the Eucharist. At a Sung Eucharist, the principles set out in ALG 3 apply (ALG 3: pp. 11–12), and the Liturgy of the Word should take place in the usual way (although see pp. 71–2, 83–4 for a consideration of how many readings should be used). Outside the context of public worship, it is sometimes difficult to balance word and sacrament. Given the understandable focus of the congregation on the baptism itself, the former can easily get overlooked. Depending on the position of the congregation and the president, to give the word its own space, it may be appropriate to use a portable legilium for the readings(s), even if the president is also the reader, and is free-standing for other parts of the rite. To emphasize its significance, candles may be placed either side of it, and it may be dressed with a hanging fall, if one is available. If the president is free-standing at the head of the nave until the Signing with the Cross, it may be best to stand in a central position, clearly visible to the congregation, and for the lectern or legilium to be placed at a slight angle to one side.

The chair

ALG 3 discusses the position of the president's chair (ALG 3: pp. 10–11). As with the lectern or ambo, at a Sung Eucharist it should be in its normal position. An exception to this may be when a number of other ministers need to be accommodated, especially if they are concelebrants (on concelebration, see ALG 3: pp. 15–18) and it would be best to move the chair to a position where they can sit either side of the president. For example, if the chair is normally placed at an angle on the north or south side of a westward-facing altar, it may be moved east of the altar so that the president and other ministers can sit behind it. This would be particularly appropriate when a bishop presides.

The altar

Once again, when initiation is celebrated within the context of a Eucharist, the altar should be in the same position, and used, as on a Sunday morning. In a non-eucharistic context, it is often a challenge to highlight the link between font and altar. This is much easier said than done. As a minimum, the altar candles should be lit. Depending on the size of the congregation, it may be possible, after baptism, for the congregation to gather round the altar, or near it, for the prayers. In Eastertide, since this is where the Easter Candle will be positioned, the baptismal candles may be lit from it at the end of the rite. At other times, it may be more convenient to light the baptismal candles at the font after the administration of baptism (see TS: p. 101, note 17), and for it to be carried to the altar by a godparent for the prayers; alternatively, the Easter Candle could lead the congregation to the altar after the baptism, carried by an assistant minister or member of the congregation, and the baptismal candle could be lit from it at the end of the rite.

8

The altar may provide a particularly appropriate setting for the Commission (see pp. 63–4), allowing the minister to explain that the newly baptized has become part of a community which gathers each week to celebrate the Eucharist, and that it is from the altar that Christians are sent out to live as Christian disciples.

Ministries

It is as important to consider ministries in connection with Christian initiation as it is in relation to the Eucharist (see ALG 3: pp. 12–19). Terms such as clergy and congregation, priest and people, ordained and lay, can easily be seen as being in opposition to each other and interpreted in a mutually exclusive way. This is a common, and unfortunate, misunderstanding. The celebrant of the rites of Christian initiation is the community of the baptized, no less than the baptized are the celebrant of the Eucharist. There is, however, one minister who, in any particular rite, administers the sacrament(s), and CW refers to that person, be they bishop, priest or deacon, as the president.

The president

The canons identify the parish priest as the normal minister of baptism (Canon B21) and the diocesan bishop as the minister of confirmation (Canon B27). Since, in the Church of England, confirmation is an episcopal rite, there is a danger that it may be perceived as of greater significance than baptism, particularly when, in the case of adult candidates, the two rites are separated.

The Liturgical Commission's commentary on the CW initiation services makes it clear that 'In an episcopally ordered church the bishop is the chief minister of the whole process of Christian initiation and is integral to its practice' (CI: p. 317). That being the case, it is unsurprising that the notes which accompany the baptism rite stipulate that 'when the bishop is present he normally presides over the whole service' (CI: p. 98, note 1). Theologically, liturgically and canonically, it is clear that, within his or her diocese, the bishop is both the 'chief pastor' (Canon C18.1) and the 'principal minister' (Canon C18.4). Pastorally, however, there will invariably be a stronger relationship between an adult candidate and their parish priest, or other minister who has been involved in preparing them for baptism and confirmation. Where this tension is felt, it is nearly always better for the bishop to delegate the baptism itself to the minister who has this pastoral relationship (CI: p. 128, note 1) than to split baptism and confirmation between two rites. Equally, as 'principal minister of word and sacrament', to give liturgical expression to the bishop's vocation to 'baptize and confirm, nurturing God's people in the life of the Spirit, and leading them in the way of holiness' (OS: p. 61), bishops should be invited to preside at the baptism of infants (even if the parish priest performs the baptism itself), at the admission of children to communion before confirmation, and at the adult catechumenal rites.

When baptism is celebrated in the context of the Eucharist, the same minister presides throughout the rite. As with an episcopal service, it is possible to delegate the baptism itself, and other elements within the rite not assigned to the president, to another minister, but the pastoral reasons for doing so are less obvious, and care must be taken not to undermine the ministry of the president. Again, the same principles apply as for the Eucharist: 'the unity of the liturgy is served by the ministry of the president, who in presiding over the whole service holds word and sacrament together and draws the congregation into a worshipping community' (CWMV: p. 158).

If there is a deacon, or a priest or lay minister exercising a diaconal role, the same principles apply as for a normal Sunday Eucharist (ALG 3: pp. 18–19). In Eastertide, they may lead the procession to and from the font, carrying the Easter Candle. They may preach and, if a deacon or priest has been particularly involved in preparing parents (and godparents) for the baptism of infants, the baptism itself may, in exceptional circumstances, be delegated to that person; in the case of lay ministers, they may preach and be invited to join in the Signing with the Cross after the Decision.

Although the canonical expectation is that the parish priest should normally administer Holy Baptism (Canon B21), deacons are also authorized to baptize, and this is common, particularly in parishes which have large numbers of 'stand-alone' baptisms, and curates or distinctive deacons are involved pastorally in baptism ministry. Liturgically, a deacon may preside over the whole rite, including saying the Prayer over the Water, but should use the *us* form of the final blessing (CI: p. 77), as at a marriage.

Vesture

Liturgical colour

White is the liturgical colour for baptism and confirmation, 'though red may be preferred' (CWMV: p. 532). Red, symbolizing the fire of the Holy Spirit, is now sometimes used at ordinations, but if initiation is linked with the paschal mystery, white would seem to be more appropriate, apart from at Pentecost and other festivals where red is the liturgical colour. At the Sunday Eucharist, the colour of the season should normally be used, and green for Ordinary Time. In the Roman Rite, red is the preferred colour for confirmation (Elliott 1995: p. 202). However, if white is used for baptism it should also be used for confirmation, so as not to imply a stronger association between the latter and the gift of the Spirit.

Initiation at the Eucharist

When initiation is celebrated at the Eucharist, the same vestments are worn by the president, deacon and other ministers as at any other eucharistic celebration.

When a bishop presides, a mitre is worn with eucharistic vestments, and the crozier is carried. In addition to the normal customs associated with episcopal presidency at the Eucharist (see ALG 3: p. 21), the mitre may be worn and the crozier held for the Presentation of the Candidates and the Decision. Although, in the Roman Rite, the bishop sits for the 'questions pertaining to the renunciation of sin and the profession of faith' (*The Ceremonial of Bishops*: p. 143) and for the presentation of candidates for confirmation (*The Ceremonial of Bishops*: p. 147), in CW, if the Presentation and Decision do not take place at the chair, it would not be appropriate to provide another chair for the bishop to use (there should not be more than one presidential chair) and, when infants are baptized, for the bishop to sit may be overly formal. At the Signing with the Cross, the bishop will need to give up the crozier, and may take it again for the procession to the font. The Prayer over the Water is said without mitre or crozier, and the bishop may take them again, or at least the mitre, for the Profession of Faith, and retain the mitre for the baptism itself.

In the Roman Rite, after the baptism of infants, the bishop sits, wearing the mitre, and recites the prescribed formulae while a priest

11

carries out the anointing, clothing and presentation of the lighted candle (*The Ceremonial of Bishops*: p. 144). Although CW could be celebrated in this way, so as not to interrupt the flow of the rite, it would seem more appropriate for the bishop to anoint with chrism, wearing the mitre, while standing at the font and, if the candidate is to be clothed, for this to happen immediately afterwards. If another minister has baptized the infant, that person should anoint the candidate. Although CW doesn't permit this prayer (CI: p. 71) to be said by anyone other than the president, if another minister has baptized and the bishop takes over to anoint, the impression given could be that the anointing is of greater significance than the baptism. Whether the Giving of a Lighted Candle and Commission take place after baptism or at the end of the rite (see pp. 65, 93–6), the bishop may wear the mitre for both, and hold the crozier for the Commission.

When presiding at confirmation, the bishop may wear the mitre to sprinkle the candidates and/or congregation (CI: p. 117), and then remove it for the prayer which follows, putting it on again and taking the crozier if there is a procession to the place of confirmation. A number of bishops still prefer to sit, wearing the mitre, to confirm. The prayer of confirmation should always be said standing, without the mitre, and it is suggested that the anointing and laying on of hands are performed in the same way (for a more detailed discussion of this, see pp. 90–3). Equally, the rites of affirmation and reception may be celebrated in this way, too.

As for assistant ministers, any concelebrating priests may wear eucharistic vestments or an alb and stole; and deacons carrying out a liturgical ministry within the rite may wear alb, stole and, if available, dalmatic. Otherwise, if clergy are robing, they should wear cotta or surplice and stole, and lay ministers should robe as they normally would at the Eucharist.

Initiation outside the Eucharist

When baptism is celebrated outside the Eucharist, the president may wear a cotta, surplice or alb with a stole. Although a cope may be worn (*Rite of Baptism for Children*: p. 15), this can present logistical problems when baptizing an infant.

When a bishop presides at the baptism of children outside the Eucharist, depending on the solemnity of the occasion, an alb, stole, cope and mitre may be worn, and the crozier carried or, more simply, an alb and stole may be worn. The former would also be suitable for celebrations of confirmation (and baptism) outside the Eucharist, including Vigil Services (CI: pp. 132–49).

Baptism by immersion

Where baptism is by immersion and the president is going to step into the water, it would be sensible to begin the service by wearing shorts under a cassock alb, with a stole and, if a Eucharist, chasuble on top. When it comes to the baptism, vestments, shoes, anything else worn on the feet, and a radio microphone, if used, should be removed, so that the president can step into the baptistery barefoot wearing the alb. After the baptism, while the candidate is dressing, the president will need to go to a room or behind a screen to remove the wet alb, dry him- or herself, and dress as before (with a new alb) before re-joining the celebration. Alternatively, if the president baptizes a candidate by immersion without stepping into the water, it may be advisable to remove the chasuble, if it is a Eucharist, and to roll up the sleeves of the alb, before doing so. (For further guidance on baptizing by immersion, see Turner 2007: pp. 103–5; Turrell 2013: pp. 92–3.)

2

Rites on the Way:
infants and children

The *Canons of the Church of England* and CW recommend that baptism should be administered 'when the most number of people come together' (see pp. xvii–xviii). If, for whatever reason, baptism is administered privately, the public celebration of rites such as the Thanksgiving for the Gift of a Child and the Welcome of Those Preparing for the Baptism of Children, presents a liturgical and pastoral opportunity to connect families to the wider Christian community. This is not to say that they are of little value when baptism is celebrated as part of public worship, but that they have greater significance for families and parishes when it is not.

Thanksgiving for the Gift of a Child

Thanksgiving for the Gift of a Child (CWMV: pp. 337–43; PS: pp. 200–12; CI: pp. 16–28) combines thanksgiving for birth or adoption, the blessing of the newborn, a public statement of the child's name, the giving of a Gospel, the opportunity for support for the child to be expressed publically by family and friends, and prayers for the child and his or her parents.

Unlike the other catechumenal rites in CW, this is an authorized rather than commended service (since it is alternative, rather than supplemental, to a rite in the Book of Common Prayer, namely 'The Churching of Women'; see CI: p. 311). This should not, however, discourage its creative use. A distinction needs to be drawn between this rite and the Welcome of Those Preparing for the Baptism of Children (CI: pp. 31–2). The latter follows the decision to have a child baptized and precedes the celebration of the sacrament, whereas the thanksgiving service can be used flexibly in a number of different ways. CW lists three: a private celebration of a birth or adoption, at home or in church; a public celebration of the same, in church but outside the context of public worship; and a public celebration of the birth or adoption of a number of children within the principal Sunday service (CI: p. 16). Although CW suggests that the rite of Welcome of Those Preparing for the Baptism of Children may be used when a child is first brought to church (CI: p. 31), it doesn't necessarily follow that this will coincide with the decision to have a child baptized. If it does, some of the thanksgiving service may be incorporated within the rite of welcome (see p. 23). If not, material from the service of thanksgiving may be more appropriate, as suggested below.

In addition to children being brought to church for the first time, who else is this service intended for? CW suggests its use as a preliminary for baptism, either when baptism follows soon afterwards, or after a longer period of time, and also that it may be used with those who 'do not ask for Baptism, but who recognize that something has happened for which they wish to give thanks to God' (CI: p. 16). Beneath this seemingly innocuous rubric lies a degree of anxiety: first, anxiety about the high demands made of parents and godparents by the baptism rite which are perceived to frighten away those who want to mark the birth of their child publically at a celebration with family and friends; and second, anxiety about baptizing the children of those who are not worshipping members of the Christian Church. In response to the second, whatever theological qualms a priest or parish may have about indiscriminate baptism, the canons are clear in respect of the expectations of the Church of England:

> No minister shall refuse or, save for the purpose of preparing or instructing the parents or guardians or godparents, delay to baptize any infant within his cure that is brought to the church to be baptized, provided that due notice has been given and the provisions relating to godparents in these Canons are observed.
>
> (*Canons of the Church of England*,
> B22.4 – Of the baptism of infants)

In relation to the first point, this is less clear-cut and, as has already been noted, Baptism Project research suggests that the strong, personal credal language of CW does not seem to deter parents from asking for baptism, nor, having had their child baptized, would they have preferred a less demanding or traditional alternative. The relative popularity of baptism over thanksgiving can be seen in the following

Church of England statistics from 2013 (infants are classified as those under the age of one, and children from one to twelve years of age):

Infant Baptism	79,420	Child Baptism	42,610
Infant Thanksgiving	4,070	Child Thanksgiving	2,040

(Research and Statistics Department of the Archbishops' Council, *Statistics for Mission 2013*)

All that said, thanksgiving for the birth or adoption of a child has an important part to play within the life of many parish communities, and is currently underutilized, particularly as a resource when children are brought to church for the first time and if baptism is to follow as a stand-alone service. It can also provide a useful framework for a rite when the child's parents come from two different faith traditions. In this case, if parents decide that the child should be given the freedom to decide in later life which tradition, if any, to follow, the service of thanksgiving is sufficiently flexible to permit the incorporation of readings and prayers from other faith traditions, alongside that which is explicitly Christian.

Introduction

The notes helpfully emphasize the importance of making clear that this is not a baptism (CI: p. 28). To avoid any confusion, it should not take place at the font; water should not be used to bless the child, and anointing would be inappropriate. If used in church, depending on the size of the congregation, the service could take place in a side chapel or in the chancel, rather than the nave. Alternatively, it may be possible to arrange some chairs around a statue or icon of the Virgin and Child, so that people can be encouraged to light candles for the child during or after the service. The minister of the rite may be ordained or lay. Although the rite is not a sacrament, a priest or deacon may wear a white stole over a cotta or surplice.

How the material is used will depend on whether the service is to be used as a stand-alone rite, either at home or in church, or incorporated into public worship. If used independently, the welcome at the beginning of the service needs to be followed by a brief explanation of what will happen. If there is a hymn, it may separate the welcome from the introduction but, given that only a few words are required for each, it may be best to join them. Although a number of liturgical greetings are provided (CI: p. 23), a more informal welcome may be more appropriate, and could lead into the introduction in the minister's own words, emphasizing thanksgiving, blessing, and prayer and support for the parents. The introduction may be followed by three congregational responses. Designed to encourage participation by all, these can fall flat, particularly if the congregation is not used to liturgical worship. It also requires the congregation to turn to an order of service which, unless there has been a hymn, will not have been required thus far, and so can disrupt the flow of the service. The introduction concludes with a simple collect. If a short period of silence is possible, the minister may invite the people to pray for the child before saying the prayer. If the minister is standing at a legilium or lectern, the *orans* position would be appropriate (see ALG 3: pp. 38–9) and the longer doxology may be added, if desired.

Reading(s) and Sermon

A Bible reading is required and several texts are suggested (CI: p. 23). A number of criteria may be used to determine which reading is used, including the liturgical season, familiarity, and the choice of the family. Given that the minister is encouraged to take the child in his or her arms later in the rite, Mark 10.13–16, despite its association with the BCP 1662 baptism of infants, may be appropriate. And if the service does take place in sight of an image of the Virgin and Child, Matthew 1.18–25, Luke 1.39–45, Luke 2.22–24; 33–40 would be suitable. If the selected passage is from the Gospels, it may be read from the copy of the Gospel which will be given later in the service. In preparing for the service, the minister may invite the parents to nominate a family member or friend to read. Alternatively, the passage may be read by a member of the ministry team or the minister. It may also be appropriate for the minister to ask the parents if they would like to include a non-biblical reading in the service. As already mentioned, this may be from another faith tradition, or it may be a piece of poetry or prose which has significance for the family. If one is included, it should be read before the Bible passage, so that the biblical reading leads into the sermon. Although CW permits the sermon to be omitted (CI: p. 28, note 5), a very short homily provides the opportunity to relate the scripture passage to the life of the child, refer to the Giving of the Gospel later in the rite, and, structurally, acts as a bridge between the reading and the thanksgiving and blessing which follow, particularly if a hymn is not sung at this point.

Thanksgiving and Blessing

At the heart of the rite are thanksgiving and blessing. Aware that some parents may like to nominate some of their family and/or friends as having a particularly significant role in the child's life and upbringing, provision is made for 'supporting friends' to stand with the parents and child for the thanksgiving (CI: p. 26, note 4). These are not godparents, and should not be described as such; although it's possible that, if a baptism follows at a later date, some or all of them may become the child's godparents. There is no requirement that they should be baptized. Their only liturgical role is the optional presentation of the child to the minister, and their response to an optional question after the Giving of the Gospel about helping and supporting the parents. Even the 'informal words' suggested by CW for the Presentation require a degree of confidence that not all supporting friends will be comfortable with. It is therefore important that this is adapted appropriately to each occasion. If the minister is asked to provide some scripted words for all the supporting friends to read, they need not be more complicated than

> We present *N* to you,
> and ask you to give thanks to God for *him*,
> and to bless *him*.

In many cases, words may be considered superfluous, and the presentation may be most clearly expressed by the friends standing with the parents.

The prayer of thanksgiving is preceded by two simple questions. Although CW does not make it clear who should answer them, parents and supporting friends may respond or, indeed, the whole congregation. It is somewhat surprising that this prayer of thanksgiving, which is central to the rite, does not mention the child by name. This may be because the optional 'naming' of the child is to follow, God is praised for the child's birth in the subsequent prayer of blessing, and there is a further opportunity for thanksgiving at the beginning of the Prayers. But if it is desired to give thanks for the child by name at this point in the service, the opening petition may be expanded. In addition, the end of the prayer may be altered so that the congregation's response is a simple 'Amen' rather than 'Blessed be God for ever', which requires the whole prayer, or at least the final line, to be printed in an order of service. An amended text could read as follows, with the second and third lines removed if a shorter text is preferred:

> God our creator,
> we thank you for the gift of *N*
> and for *his* family and friends.
> We thank you for all whose support and skill
> surround and sustain the beginning of life.
> We thank you that we are known to you by name
> and loved by you from all eternity.
> We thank you for Jesus Christ,
> who has opened to us the way of love.
> We praise you, Father, Son, and Holy Spirit,
> now and for evermore.

All **Amen.**

As for the naming, if this form of the thanksgiving is used, it makes little sense to ask for the child's name after it has already been mentioned in prayer. The question and its response, by a parent or supporting friend, may be transposed so that it precedes the two questions at the beginning of the Thanksgiving and Blessing. If the service is being used for more than one child, the opening question will need to be asked separately of each child, and the other two used for all of them collectively.

The rite then moves from thanksgiving to blessing. A parent or supporting friend may hand the child to the minister. If more than one child is to be blessed, the minister may hold each child in turn and repeat the prayer at the bottom of page 19 of CI. If another minister is present, that person may hold the book during the blessing, or a parent or supporting friend can be asked to assist. During the blessing, the minister may lay a hand on the baby's head, and/or make the sign of the cross over him or her. Given its association with the liturgy of baptism, making the sign of the cross on the child's forehead would be inappropriate. After the blessing, the child may be returned to a parent or supporting friend to hold during the congregational prayer which follows. Since it is not optional, its reference to the child coming 'through faith and baptism' to the fullness of God's grace is curious in a rite which may be used for those who do not wish to have their child baptized (CI: p. 16). In some contexts, particularly when one parent is of another faith, it may be appropriate to delete 'come through faith and baptism'. The use of a congregational prayer requires it to be printed in an order of service. If this is not possible, or if literacy is an issue, the minister may say the words alone while continuing to hold the child. This part of the rite concludes with a blessing of the parents, during which the minister may repeat the ritual gesture used for the child, laying a hand on their heads, and/or making the sign of the cross over them.

Giving of the Gospel

A copy of one of the Gospels, possibly that which was used for the reading, may be given to a parent or supporting friend. It would be appropriate for a bookplate, signed by the minister, to be placed inside the front cover, and for it to include a quotation from the reading and/or a prayer for the child and parents.

The questions to the supporting friends, and wider family and friends, which follow, are optional. If they are used, and a simple response is required, it would suffice for them to say 'We will' or even 'Yes'. Once the congregation have publically expressed their support for the family, the service moves naturally into the prayers.

Prayers

The prayers begin with an optional prayer which may be said by the parents or by the whole congregation. Its use by the parents alone will require them to feel sufficiently confident and to participate in this way. If it is not used, the text can be easily adapted so that it can be said by the minister for the parents, and it may be supplemented by some of the additional prayers that are provided (CI: pp. 24–7). If the minister wishes to adapt the form on page 21 of CI, it may be done as follows:

> God our creator,
> we thank you for the gift of *N*
> entrusted to the care of *N* and *N*.
> May they be patient and understanding,
> ready to guide and to forgive,
> so that through their love
> *N* may come to know your love;
> through Jesus Christ our Lord.

All **Amen.**

If there is an image of the Virgin and Child near the place where the service takes place, the parents and supporting friends can be invited to pray for the child by lighting a candle at it, and other members of the congregation can be invited to do the same at the end of the service.

The Prayers conclude with the Lord's Prayer, for which it may be helpful to have a text available.

Ending

The minister concludes the service with an appropriate blessing of the congregation, for which two possible texts are provided. A lay minister or deacon changes the words in italics to the first person plural.

CW directs that a register should be kept (not the baptism register), recording the names of the children for whom this service has been used, and that they should be given a certificate (CI: p. 28, note 1). Several designs can be found in Brind and Wilkinson 2010 (pp. 54–9).

Thanksgiving for the Gift of a Child during public worship

Material from this service can easily be used within public worship. Although the rite makes clear that it may be used 'as part of a main Sunday act of worship' (CI: p. 16), no guidance is given as to how this may be done. Given that it may sometimes be the case that the president or officiating minister will not know in advance that the child is likely to make its first appearance on a particular Sunday, and that adding a number of additional liturgical elements may overload the rite, 'less is more' is probably the best advice here. At its simplest, the prayer of blessing in CI at the bottom of page 19 may be sufficient, continuing, possibly, with either or both of the next two prayers. As to when this should happen, these may be incorporated as part of the notices or between the intercessions and the Peace; if the latter, the child can be welcomed by the congregation during the Peace. If a Gospel is to be given, it could be a version of that from which the Gospel of the Day has been read.

If parents who are members of the congregation have decided that they want their child to choose whether or not to be baptized when he or she is older, and would therefore like a public thanksgiving within the main Sunday service, other elements of the thanksgiving rite may be incorporated between the sermon and the intercessions.

If a child of parents who are regular members of the congregation is to be baptized elsewhere (for example, the church in which the parents were married, or where there is a strong family connection), elements from the thanksgiving service may be included within the service they normally attend on a convenient Sunday some time before the baptism.

If it is the parish's policy for most baptisms (or, at least, those of children from families which are not regular churchgoers) to take place outside the main Sunday liturgy, it may be appropriate to include a rite of thanksgiving monthly or bimonthly at an all-age service, and invite the parents of children to be baptized in the next few weeks to attend along with any family or friends who are able to join them. This can be seen as part of their preparation for baptism, and enables them to be introduced to the worshipping community. Although the Welcome of Those Preparing for the Baptism of Children is intended for this purpose, a rite with a greater emphasis on thanksgiving and celebration may be more appropriate; alternatively, elements from the thanksgiving can be combined with the rite of welcome (see p. 23).

Thanksgiving for the Gift of a Child in hospital or at home

A minister visiting a mother and child in hospital or at home may wish to use a prayer of thanksgiving and blessing, particularly after a difficult birth (for which a prayer is provided in CI: p. 26). If a couple has recently moved into a new home, a priest may be invited to bless the house. In such cases, material from the thanksgiving may be incorporated (see, for example, the 'Celebration for a Home' in the BOS: pp. 146–56).

Pastoral adaptations

The minister will need to be sensitive to individual family circumstances and adjust the rite as appropriate (see CI: p. 28, notes 2 and 3). Thanksgiving and prayer for family and friends who have died may sometimes be appropriate. If so, the congregation can be encouraged to light candles for them, as well as for the child. It is becoming more common for couples to ask for the baptism of their child or children, or thanksgiving for them, to take place at the same time as their marriage. For the Liturgical Commission's guidance on how to combine the rites, see <www.churchofengland.org/media/1180798/marriagebaptismthanksgiving.pdf>.

Welcome of Those Preparing for the Baptism of Children

The register of the language in this short rite is quite different from the Thanksgiving for the Gift of a Child and, unsurprisingly, bears a much closer resemblance to baptism. As has already been suggested, it may be more appropriate to use it within public worship with those who are regular members of the congregation than with families who are less familiar with the Church's liturgy. CW suggests that it may also be used more informally as part of baptism preparation (CI: p. 31), though if it is hoped that the rite will enable the congregation to express its welcome and support, the principal Sunday liturgy is likely to provide the best opportunity to do so, perhaps during an all-age service.

It begins with the congregation being asked to express its welcome and support, followed by a question to parents and godparents, if any are present, asking them if they will 'pray for *these children*, and help *them* to grow in the knowledge and love of God and to take *their* place in the life and worship of the Church'. Next comes a prayer for children and parents, and the rite concludes with the optional commissioning and blessing of godparents. Overall, this rite strikes a less celebratory note than the previous service of thanksgiving. To remedy this, the prayers of thanksgiving and blessing from the other rite could be incorporated, together with the Giving of the Gospel, between the question to the congregation and that to the parents and godparents (CI: p. 31), although this will add to the overall length of the service, and perhaps make it more wordy than it needs to be.

CW suggests that it may be inserted before the prayers of intercession, at the Peace, or before the dismissal. Since it is desirable for the rite to lead into a more informal welcome of the family, to position it before the Peace would be appropriate. Whenever it happens, the family should be asked to join the minister at the front of the church and face the congregation. Alternatively, if the family is sitting together, the minister can go to them, and invite the rest of the congregation to turn to face them. If godparents are to be commissioned, it would be appropriate for the minister to extend his or her right hand over them during the first part of the prayer of blessing, making the sign of the cross as the Trinity is invoked. In response, the 'Amen' should be said, if possible, by the godparents, and not by the minister alone.

Admission of the Baptized to Communion

The admission of children to communion before confirmation is a wide-ranging and complex issue, the history of which has already been touched upon (see pp. xiii–xvi). The focus of this section is how the rite of Admission of the Baptized to Communion may be used (CI: pp. 188–92). In addition to the official regulations, each Church of England diocese has its own guidelines on the process of admitting children to communion, which are normally accompanied by a list of suggested resources.

The notes provide helpful, common-sense advice both on how to prepare for the admission of children to communion (on which, see also Earey 2007: pp. 75–7), and on how the provision might be used. The regulations do not require there to be any rite of admission, but it would be odd not to celebrate this significant moment in the life of the individual and the community publically and liturgically.

The notes recommend that a clear distinction should be made between this rite and the celebration of Christian initiation. To this end, the use of water, oil and the laying on of hands should not be used (CI: p. 188, note 3). For the same reason, it would be inadvisable for children to be admitted to communion within an initiation service. Rather if, as CW suggests (CI: p. 188, note 4), it is to take place at a main Sunday service, it would be best for this to be an all-age eucharistic liturgy at which children are present throughout. Where some of those to be admitted normally sing in a choir or serve, on this occasion it may be more appropriate for them to sit in the congregation with family, friends, godparents, others to be admitted and those who have been involved in preparing them for their first communion. To highlight their presence, the candidates could walk with the ministers in the entrance procession. To emphasize that it is on the basis of their baptism that they are being admitted to communion, they could be invited to carry their baptismal candles. If any of the candidates no longer have them, or one was not given at their baptism, another could be provided for use on this occasion and to keep (given before, rather than during, the service, to avoid any confusion with baptism). Having entered, the candles could be placed in holders on the altar (depending on the number of candidates and size of the altar), or in a pricket stand or tray of sand set up so that it is visible to the congregation.

CW provides a helpful Pastoral Introduction. It is not intended that it should be read aloud at the service, but it could usefully inform the president's introduction to the Eucharist, or be printed in an order of service or notice sheet. CW provides two forms of welcome, which may be used at the Greeting or before the Peace (CI: p. 188, note 5). Since it is likely that the sermon or talk will refer to the significance of the occasion, it's probably best to delay it until the Peace, so that the liturgy can build towards that moment. In the first form, those to be admitted should stand with the president in front of the congregation as they are introduced using the text provided, or in the president's own words. If the CW formula is used, concluding with '*N and N*, we welcome you in Jesus' name to receive communion with us', although no response is provided, it would be appropriate for the congregation to affirm what the president has said by responding '**We welcome you**' and then applauding.

A second form of admission is entitled 'The Questions' (CI: p. 192). This may only be used before the Peace and consists of two questions, first to the congregation and then to the candidates, and a prayer. This form has the advantage of enabling the congregation to express their support of the children, and the children themselves to articulate their desire to receive communion. Its disadvantage is that it lacks the strength of welcome which the first form provides. Parishes need to assess the relative merits of each in their individual contexts.

In addition to the admission, CW also provides appropriate forms of the Peace, Preparation of the Table, Proper Preface, Post Communion and Dismissal. A bidding for use in the Prayers of Intercession is also given, and it is suggested that one of the forms of prayer on pages 53–5, the Profession of Faith from the baptism rite and the Affirmation of the Christian Way (CI: p. 36) may be suitable (CI: p. 188, note 6). Given the presence of young children, and the need for the liturgy to be as inclusive of them as possible, the length of some of these texts, the complexity of their language and the theological concepts they express may make them sit uncomfortably within an all-age liturgy. For this reason, the use of the alternative Profession of Faith (CI: p. 178), and one of the Additional Eucharistic Prayers (2012), may be considered appropriate, although it's important that the service does not depart too much from the normal pattern of an all-age Eucharist. If Eucharistic Prayer G is used, the following may replace the bracketed intercession:

Bless with Christ's presence *those* who make their first communion
   today.
Strengthen *them* as they seek to follow Christ
and help *them* to put their trust in him for ever.

Whichever texts are used, consideration also needs to be given to appropriate ritual involvement. At the offertory, those newly admitted may assist with the collection, if there is one, and bring the gifts of bread and wine to the altar. During the Eucharistic Prayer, they may stand around the altar, moving to the normal position for the administration of communion, and receiving before other members of the congregation. If they carried candles during the entrance procession, they may be given back to them during the final hymn, and the new communicants may join the procession as it leaves, walking with the ministers.

The 2006 Regulations require the incumbent to maintain a register of all children admitted to Holy Communion. The incumbent is also required to record on the child's baptismal certificate their first admission to communion or, if that's not possible, prepare a certificate with details of their first communion (para. 9). So as not to lengthen the service, these may be given to the children and their parents afterwards.

3

Rites on the Way: adults

The genius of the catechumenate approach to evangelism is that it combines teaching (catechesis) and worship in an accompanied process of Christian formation. Consideration of how any liturgical rites might be used to accompany a person's journey towards baptism needs to go hand in hand with careful thought about what form the catechesis itself should take. Divided into two stages, one of the strengths of Pilgrim (see p. x) is that it is not limited to those preparing for baptism (or, indeed, confirmation, or any other rite of affirmation). The Follow stage is for those who are new to the faith (which may include those baptized as infants who have since lapsed), while the Grow stage is for those who want to take things further (either those who have completed the first stage, and now want to go on, or those who have been Christians for some time and are seeking renewal in their faith). This chapter will consider how Rites on the Way may be used alongside Pilgrim for catechumens and, where appropriate, for others. That these services should be used in this broad way is affirmed by the Liturgical Commission's commentary:

> These services seek to recognize that journey and pattern are integral to the Christian life and need to be reflected in any approach to Christian initiation. They offer a framework to help new disciples find their feet in our shared Christian life. They are also offered as aids for all God's people to help explore the identity and calling that are ours in Christ. They complement the other Initiation services.
>
> (CI: p. 326)

Liturgical pathways

Part of the reason why the CW material is so extensive is that it needs to accommodate individuals travelling along different pathways and with different goals, as well as communities with varying needs and traditions. Although some of those who begin to explore the Christian faith may have had no previous experience of the Church, others may have been baptized as infants, but never attended church since; and still others may have been regular worshippers at one time in their lives (and perhaps also been confirmed) but then fallen away.

In attempting to enable the Christian community to accompany people whose journey takes them along these various pathways, CW provides **two** principal rites:

1 The *Welcome* of Disciples on the Way of Faith (CI: pp. 33–5).
2 The *Call* and Celebration of the Decision to be Baptized or Confirmed or to Affirm Baptismal Faith (CI: pp. 37–9)

The Welcome is for 'those who, after initial exploration of the Christian faith, wish to learn the Christian Way within the life of the people of God' (CI: p. 33). These are not initial enquirers, those who have just signed up for Pilgrim, or who have been attending church for a few weeks, but 'those who want to commit themselves to continuing the journey of faith' (p. 33). Within Pilgrim, it is suggested that this may be appropriate on completion of the first Follow course (Croft 2013, *Pilgrim: Leader's Guide*, p. 56). In RCIA, which retains much of the patristic terminology, this is known as the rite of Acceptance into the Order of Catechumens. In the Church of England, this moment may be an appropriate time for clergy and lay leaders (catechists) to think about when individual members of the group may be ready for an initial discussion about which pathway (towards baptism, confirmation or affirmation), if any, they may wish to follow.

The Call may take place several months or more after the Welcome. The Toronto Statement describes this transitional phase not as a 'period of probation' for the candidates 'to see whether their discipleship matches up to certain criteria', but rather as a 'period of growth and discernment in which both individual and church are involved' (Holeton 1993: p. 239). As a result, the Call is much more focused than the Welcome, and gives liturgical expression to a significant staging-point reached by a candidate with the support of the church: the decision to be baptized or confirmed, or to publically affirm baptismal faith. In RCIA, this is the Election or Enrolment of Names, during which 'catechumens' become the 'elect'.

Among the other catechumenal material, the most significant is The Presentation of the Four Texts (CI: pp. 40–7). Imitating early church practice in which the Apostles' Creed and the Lord's Prayer were handed over (*traditio symboli*) to catechumens so that they could be learnt and then read aloud by the candidates (*redditio symboli*) before their baptism, CW has identified these and a further two texts, Jesus' Summary of the Law and the Beatitudes, as a basis for catechesis. Pilgrim contains material focusing on each so that, once again, worship and catechesis may be combined in the process of formation.

Other supplementary liturgical material includes an *Affirmation of the Christian Way* (CI: p. 36) and some prayers for use in preparation for baptism (pp. 48–9). The latter could appropriately be used at the end of a baptism rehearsal. CW also provides a selection of classic prayers for use with 'learning groups' (CI: pp. 51–2), such as Pilgrim, forms of intercession that would be appropriate at a Sunday Eucharist (CI: pp. 53–5), forms of the Preparation of the Table, Dismissal, and a text to use when a Bible is presented to someone exploring the faith (CI: p. 56).

Rites on the Way and the Christian year

It is the intention of CW that these rites should be 'most appropriately celebrated by the whole community when placed within particular sections of the cycle of the Christian year' (CI: pp. 5–6). Three are highlighted: the Epiphany/Baptism of Christ; Easter/Pentecost; and All Saints' tide. This seasonal approach is commended as follows:

> Rites on the Way support a journey of faith which in some ways mirrors the story of Jesus as it is told by the Christian community through the seasons. It is therefore appropriate to use the seasons to enhance the sense of journey and of the climax to that journey which is already firmly within the historical understanding of the faith.
>
> (CI: p. 330)

CW provides three patterns which outline how the various rites, beginning with the Call, might be distributed within particular seasons (CI: pp. 331–3). In each case, there is a Sunday set aside for the Call, four Sundays for the *traditio* of each of the four texts, another Sunday for the celebration of the sacraments of initiation, and a final liturgical celebration of Thanksgiving for Holy Baptism (CI: pp. 184–7), which may include the Commission and Sending Out (CI: p. 331). Even if this pattern is only celebrated once a year, or once every two or three years, many may feel that, no matter how significant initiation is in the life of the Church, to give over seven principal services to its celebration within a short space of time may be too much for the candidates and, indeed, the parish, to cope with. This may be another reason why these Rites on the Way are currently so infrequently used.

It is important to emphasize that it is not necessary to use all of the rites provided every time an adult is baptized, confirmed, or affirms baptismal faith. Indeed, it may almost always be preferable not to! Nor is it essential to have a public, liturgical *traditio* of all four of the texts. If a cut has to be made, the Apostles' Creed and Lord's Prayer should always take precedence. The table opposite outlines a more streamlined approach which attempts to retain the seasonal emphasis and the interaction with the Sunday worshipping community without being overly burdensome.

If it is desired to reduce this further, the presentation of either or both of the Apostles' Creed and Lord's Prayer may take place as part of the worship at the beginning of the study group in which the text will be discussed in the weeks preceding the celebration of initiation.

The same seasonal approach is taken by Pilgrim, which adopts an agricultural model divided into seasons of Sowing, Nurture, Growth and Prayer, roughly mirroring the first of the patterns outlined above, the rite of Welcome taking place at the beginning of Advent (Croft 2013, *Pilgrim: A Leader's Guide*, pp. 28–32).

Rites on the Way and the local community

In deciding which pattern to follow, local factors should always be taken into account, not least the number of candidates. It is undoubtedly easier to run Pilgrim courses in tandem with the celebration of Rites on the Way when there is enough interest to make it viable for those who run them and sufficiently non-threatening for those who participate. In multi-parish benefices, it may be possible to run a group for the whole benefice rather than individual parishes, and for at least some of the liturgical celebrations to take place on occasions when the whole benefice worships together in one place. Evidence suggests that Pilgrim courses have been well received in a number of parishes of different traditions across the Church. From the perspective of this guide, there remains a twofold challenge: how to integrate catechesis within public worship; and how to establish and develop a relationship between catechumenal groups and Sunday congregations.

Table 3.1 The celebration of Rites on the Way and initiation at Easter, Epiphany and All Saints

Pattern 1	*Initiation at Easter*
Call	First Sunday of Lent
Presentation of the Creed and Lord's Prayer	Two Sundays of Lent
Baptism, Confirmation (if bishop presides), Affirmation, Reception	Easter Vigil or Easter Day A weekday Eucharist between
Thanksgiving and Sending Out	Ascension and Pentecost

Pattern 2	*Initiation at Epiphany /Baptism of Christ*
Call	First Sunday of Advent
Presentation of the Creed and Lord's Prayer	Two Sundays between the Second Sunday of Advent and the First/ Second Sunday of Christmas
Baptism, Confirmation (if bishop presides), Affirmation, Reception	Epiphany or, The Baptism of Christ
Thanksgiving and Sending Out	A weekday Eucharist on or near the feast of the Conversion of St Paul (25 January)

(The reference to the 'Fifth Sunday of Advent' (CI: p. 332) is an error!)

Pattern 3	*Initiation at All Saints*
Call	Holy Cross Day (14 September) or the nearest Sunday
Presentation of the Creed and Lord's Prayer	Two of the last four Sundays after Trinity
Baptism, Confirmation (if bishop presides), Affirmation, Reception	All Saints' Day (1 November) or All Saints' Sunday
Thanksgiving and Sending Out	A weekday Eucharist on or near the feast of St Andrew (30 November)

Those exploring the way of Christ are involved in an accompanied journey of faith. Sponsors (see CI: p. 29, note 1, and p. 342) play an important part in this. CW suggests, 'At the Welcome, the new disciple should agree with the minister on a member of the church to be their companion and supporter, and to act as their sponsor' (CI: p. 29).

That said, the welcome and support of the wider congregation is just as important, and often much more difficult to achieve! The Toronto Statement sees 'the catechumenal process affirming and celebrating the baptismal identity of the whole community' (Holeton 1993: p. 236). New disciples are part of the community's life and should be prayed for regularly, not just on the Sundays when something is happening to them in the liturgy. In the early Church, the catechumenate was punctuated by frequent exorcisms accompanied by the laying on of hands. In our contemporary context, from time to time, members of the group may be invited forward before the blessing to kneel (perhaps at the altar rail) while sponsors and group leaders lay hands on them, and the president, with hands extended, prays using these or similar words:

> Father, we thank you for the call of Christ
> and for all who seek to follow him:
> support with your grace and protection
> these your servants who have set themselves to learn
>   the Way of Christ;
> as they continue to discern your will
> may they know your love
> and be a source of life to others.
> This we ask through Christ our Lord.

All **Amen.**   (CI: p. 54, adapted)

Prayer cards could also be produced for members of the congregation to take away to remind them to pray for the group during the week.

Welcome of Disciples on the Way of Faith

Whereas RCIA's rite for Acceptance into the Order of Catechumens may only be used for those preparing for baptism, and BOS provides a rite for catechumens proper (BOS: pp. 117–19) and another for the Preparation of Baptized Persons for Reaffirmation of the Baptismal Covenant (BOS: pp. 139–41), CW adopts a one-size-fits-all approach with its rite of Welcome of Disciples on the Way of Faith. This has advantages and disadvantages. Its main advantage is that it allows all those participating in a Pilgrim course, or similar, who wish to be welcomed publically, to be welcomed at the same service, thus strengthening the group's identity both among its members and in the eyes of the congregation. The flip side of this is that it can be a challenge to distinguish between those already baptized and those not. Since the rite makes no assumption as to what pathway any individual member of the group might be following, this may not be such an issue at this stage in the process, if the president is sensitive to avoid making reference to 'becoming members of the church', if some of the group are already baptized, and is careful to use the correct formula when signing the candidates' foreheads (CI: pp. 34–5).

CW does not provide a fully worked-out order of service, but a rite to be inserted into a rite, and for this reason there is no structure page. In order to understand the logic of the rite, it is helpful to note that, under the subheading 'Welcome', it consists of:

- the church welcoming the candidates;
- the candidates expressing their desire to 'learn the Way of Christ';
- the congregation promising to support the candidates;
- the sponsors expressing their support and, optionally, being commissioned;
- the candidates being signed with the cross;
- prayer being offered for each candidate.

This rite of Welcome is intended to be used during an act of public worship (CI: p. 33, note 2). In many parishes this will be the Sunday Eucharist. It is suggested that it may be used before the Collect, after the sermon or before the Peace. BOS stipulates after the sermon or the Creed (BOS: p. 117). However, given CW's emphasis on welcome, the Gathering would seem to be the most obvious and appropriate point. CW also suggests that 'the rite might begin outside the church building or at the church door' (CI: p. 33, note 2). The layout of the building will affect how this is done. If the font is at the west end of the church and the main door nearby, one possibility would be for the candidates to wait with their sponsors by the main door, and for the procession to go to the font/west end of the church during the entrance hymn so that the Gathering can begin from there.

The Welcome may be inserted after the Greeting. The congregation needs to be able to see the candidates. They and their sponsors should therefore come to stand facing the people with their backs to the font and/or door and the president should turn to face the candidates (with his or her back to the rest of the congregation) when they are being addressed. It is important to note that the candidates are being introduced to the whole community, not just the president. The sponsors' words of introduction need be no more elaborate than: 'Brothers and sisters, it's my pleasure to introduce N, and to ask you to join me in welcoming *him*' (adaptation will be necessary if the candidate is already well known to the congregation). Theologically, it is significant that the welcome precedes any commitment which the candidates are asked to make, and that it is explicit in the rite that God is already at work in the candidates' lives, and that it is his grace which has brought them to this time and place. When asked what they seek, most candidates are likely to prefer the response provided, which may be said individually, after they have been introduced, rather than using their own words.

If sponsors are to be commissioned, they may stand together in front of the president after they have expressed their support for the candidates (CI: p. 34). If a server or another minister is available to hold the book, the president may extend his or her hands, palms down, over the sponsors while saying the prayer, and make the sign of the cross in blessing at the end. The 'Amen' should be said by the sponsors rather than the president.

When it comes to the Signing with the Cross, although CW permits the question to be addressed to the group together, it is probably best to address each candidate separately (unless there is a very large number of them), and for them to be signed as soon as they have answered 'I will'. This is the central moment of the rite, and will have greater significance for the candidates if it can be done individually. Since, in the Church of England, the use of the oil of baptism (often referred to as the oil of catechumens) is associated with the pre-baptismal anointing, and this rite is not a precursor to baptism, oil is not used for this consignation. Two formulas are provided, one for use with catechumens and the other with those who have already been baptized. Sponsors are invited to express their support of the candidates by signing them after the president. The rite concludes with prayer being offered for each new disciple. With the sponsors placing a hand on the shoulder of their candidate, the president may say the prayer provided with hands extended towards the candidates (as in the earlier commissioning). Alternatively, the president may lay hands on each while praying for them silently, the sponsor's hand resting on the candidate's shoulder. A simple chant may accompany this. Once hands have been laid on all the candidates, the president, with hands extended, may use the prayer provided to conclude the rite. The candidates may kneel for the prayer, if this is possible, or remain standing.

As the Eucharist continues, the Prayers of Penitence may be omitted altogether, or inserted between the intercessions and the Peace. The entrance procession resumes during the Gloria, the candidates and their sponsors following and joining family and friends, wherever they are sitting. If incense is used, it may be put on before the procession sets off, and the altar may be censed during the Gloria, which is followed by the Collect.

When it comes to the Eucharistic Prayer, if CW Prayer G is used, prayer for the new disciples may be offered within the optional intercession:

> Remember, Lord, *N* and *N*
> whom we have welcomed as *disciples* on the Way of Christ.
> May your Spirit be *their* companion and guide
> and fill *them* with the knowledge of your love.
> Give us grace to support one another
> and bring us all at the last with . . .

A final rubric suggests that 'a gift expressing welcome to the new disciple from the congregation may be given'. Suggestions of what this might be are given (CI: p. 30, note 3). So as not to interrupt the rite, the most appropriate place for the giving of gifts may be during any notices which are given before the blessing.

Affirmation of the Christian Way

This short responsorial affirmation (CI: p. 36) asks Christ, the Way, to guide his people on their journey. It is suggested that this may be used in public worship to highlight the presence of those exploring the faith, or in a more informal setting. If used as part of the rites of Welcome or Call at the Sunday Eucharist, or on another appropriate occasion, such as the Sunday preceding the celebration of the sacraments of initiation, it may be led from the baptistery and inserted before the Blessing and Dismissal, the procession having moved to the font, with the candidate(s), during the final hymn. CI notes that 'it may be led by two or three people'. If desired, these could include adults who have been baptized in recent years and/or the candidates' sponsors. Pilgrim suggests that, if baptism and confirmation are celebrated outside the candidates' own parish, it may be incorporated into a service of Celebration (CI: pp. 182–3; see Chapter 6, pp. 103–4) at the principal service the following Sunday before the final blessing (Croft 2013, *Pilgrim: A Leader's Guide*, p. 63).

Call and Celebration of the Decision to the Baptized or Confirmed or to Affirm Baptismal Faith

This rite is 'intended for those who wish to continue on the Way, following a period of exploration and regular involvement in the Christian community' (CI: p. 37, note 1). Within the timetable envisaged by Pilgrim, this would most naturally happen at the end of the second of the Follow courses, at the beginning of Lent. In this rite, so as not to undermine the significance and centrality of baptism, it is important to maintain a clear distinction between any candidates who wish to be baptized and others who wish to be confirmed or affirm their baptismal faith. Once again, this is not an issue for RCIA, whose rite of Election or Enrolment of Names is only for those preparing for baptism. In America, BOS has an RCIA-style rite of Enrolment (BOS: pp. 122–6) and a separate Enrolment for Lenten Preparation (BOS: pp. 141–3) for candidates for confirmation, affirmation and reception. In order to distinguish between the two groups of candidates, it is recommended that the latter take place on Ash Wednesday, and the former on the First Sunday of Lent. Turrell, however, suggests that they should be combined in the same Sunday liturgy, while keeping the two groups distinct (Turrell 2013: p. 62). Whereas CW is not as restrictive as BOS in terms of when the rite happens, it does stipulate that 'the Call should be included in an act of public worship, and may be used before the collect, after the sermon or before the peace' (CI: p. 37, note 2).

Under the heading 'Call and Celebration', the structure of the rite is as follows:

- the church welcoming the candidates;
- the candidates expressing the desire to 'follow the Way of Christ;'
- optional testimony of sponsors and enrolment of names;
- the candidates being signed with the cross with optional anointing;
- presentation of a copy of a Gospel;
- prayers of intercession.

What is immediately striking is how similar this is to the rite of Welcome, much more so than the parallel rites in RCIA and BOS, in which the liturgical focal point of the first rite is the Signing with the Cross, and of the second the enrolment of names. Given their similarity in CW, they are often confused, and the apparent similarity may cause difficulty when preparing candidates for them. Liturgically and pastorally they need to be distinct, and this can be achieved in a number of ways without omitting the second signing. First, in terms of when in the rite the Call takes place, since it leads into the prayers of intercession, it would make sense for it to follow the Creed (this will also enable the preacher to refer to what is about to happen), and for it to happen at the front of church, rather than at the font, as suggested for the Welcome. The rite should include the enrolment of the names of any candidates for baptism in a book (see below), and candidates for baptism should be anointed. These last two suggestions will also help to maintain a distinction between those preparing for baptism and other candidates.

After the Creed, the president introduces the rite and invites the disciples and their sponsors to stand in front of him or her. At this point, it is probably best for the disciples and their sponsors to face the congregation with their backs to the altar, and for the president to stand between them and the congregation. The rite notes two occasions when the sponsors may wish to talk about the candidates in their own words: as they present them to the congregation following the president's welcome, and when the disciples have affirmed their commitment to follow the Way of Christ. To avoid unnecessary repetition, thought needs to be given to how this can be concise, while retaining a sense of the personal. In the logic of the rite, the sponsors need to 'confirm the candidates' commitment to worship, prayer and the fellowship of the Church, and their readiness to study and to understand their story as part of the people of God' (CI: p. 38) once the candidates have indicated that it is their wish to follow Christ. For this reason, the presentation and the confirmation of commitment cannot easily be combined. One way of doing this is for the opening presentation to be a simple

> Brothers and sisters, I present to you *N*
> who wishes to be baptized / confirmed / affirm *his* baptismal faith

and for the sponsor to use his or her own words to talk briefly about the candidates' commitment at the later point.

If the group of disciples includes those to be baptized, as well as those preparing for confirmation/affirmation, it may be helpful to treat them separately. The president welcomes all the candidates on behalf of the community. Candidates for confirmation and affirmation stand to one side as those preparing for baptism are presented by their sponsors. After expressing the desire to follow Christ (using the formula provided or their own words), the president asks a further question, 'Do you wish to be baptized?', to which they respond together, 'I do'. If the candidates use their own words at this point, they should be encouraged to mention that they wish to be baptized, so that the second question can be omitted. Sponsors may then confirm their candidate's commitment (see above), after which the president says to all the candidates:

> In the name of God, and with the support of your *sponsors*,
> I accept you as *candidates* for Baptism,
> and direct that your *names* be written in this book.
> May *they* also be written in the Book of Life.
>
> (BOS: p. 123, adapted)

The candidates then write their names in a book kept for this purpose, in which has been printed something approximating:

> The Parish of [insert name]
> [insert name of Sunday and year]
> In the name of God, and with the support of *their sponsors*,
> [leave space for names of candidates to be written]
> *were* accepted as *candidates* for Baptism.

The candidates write their names in the space provided, and the president signs at the bottom of the page. If there are several candidates, a chant, song, hymn or short anthem may be sung while this happens. The president then asks each candidate in turn if they will receive the sign of the cross. At this point it would be helpful if a server or other minister could hold the book for the president, while someone else approaches with the oil of baptism. If possible, this should be stored in a glass cruet or jug which, before the beginning of the service, is placed on a table so that it is visible to the congregation. The oil can now be poured into the palm of the president's hand or a shallow bowl, and taken from there to anoint. In response to the president's question, each candidate replies 'I will', and the president anoints the candidate on the forehead with the sign of the cross. As the president

38

moves on to the next candidate, the previous candidate's sponsor may also sign their candidate with oil silently. (For further discussion of anointing in this rite, see ALG 4: pp. 44–5.) If candidates for baptism are anointed at the Call they are not anointed again at the pre-baptismal Signing with the Cross in the baptism rite (CI: p. 37, note 3).

Once all the candidates for baptism have been anointed, they move to one side and the other candidates come to stand in front of the president. A lavabo may be needed at this point to wash the president's hands. The candidates are presented by their sponsors, and then affirm their desire to follow Christ, using their own words or the formula provided. Their sponsors may testify to their commitment before the president asks them individually if they wish to follow Christ. After they answer, the president signs them with the cross (without oil) on the forehead using the second formula (CI: p. 39), followed by the sponsor.

Once these candidates have been signed, they are joined by the candidates for baptism to form one group. The president is given the Book of the Gospels, holds it up, so that it is clearly visible to the candidates, and says the formula in CI, page 39. At this point, each sponsor may give to their candidate a copy of one of the Gospels, preferably the one being read in that year's Sunday lectionary cycle. The candidates then turn to face the congregation as the president introduces the intercessions. One of the forms on pages 39 or 53–5 may be used, led by a sponsor or another member of the congregation. After the final bidding, the intercessor may introduce a period of silence, which the president may conclude with the prayer of St Benedict (CI: p. 52) or another suitable prayer.

As with the Welcome, when it comes to the Eucharistic Prayer, the following may be inserted into Prayer G:

> Remember, Lord, *N* and *N*
> whom you have called to follow Christ.
> As they continue on their journey,
> defend them from evil
> and give them hope in the promise of salvation.
> Give us grace to support one another
> and bring us all at the last with . . .

(For suggestions on how to celebrate the Call in different seasons, see ALG 5: pp. 102–4.)

The Presentation of the Four Texts

The liturgical material provided to accompany the presentation of each of these texts facilitates the integration of worship and catechesis. As has already been mentioned, careful thought needs to be given about how many of the texts will be presented, as well as whether the presentation should take place during public worship or at the beginning of the study group in which they will be discussed. Traditionally, the Apostles' Creed was handed over on the Third Sunday of Lent and the Lord's Prayer two weeks later. Guidance will be given here on the *traditio* of these two texts (making use of material from CW and BOS), whether it takes place in Lent or at another time in the year. This rite is not limited to those preparing for baptism.

After the sermon, the president invites the candidates and their sponsors to stand facing the congregation. The president faces the congregation and may say:

> Brothers and sisters, let us pray for N and N who *are* preparing to be baptized, and for N and N who *are* preparing to be confirmed/renew *their* baptismal faith.

The candidates bow their heads (or kneel, if that is possible), and the sponsors each place a hand on their candidate's shoulder. Silence is kept. A server or other ministers holds the book for the president, who may pray, facing the candidates with hands outstretched:

> Lord Christ, true Light who enlightens everyone:
> shine, we pray, in the *hearts* of *these candidates*,
> that *they* may clearly see the way that leads to eternal life,
> and may follow it without stumbling;
> for you are the Way, O Christ, the Truth and the Life,
> now and for ever.
>
> *All* **Amen.**   (BOS: p. 127, adapted)

The president then introduces the presentation of the text (CI: pp. 44, 42), after which the congregation recites the text in the form that is normally used in public worship in that community. With hands held in the *orans* position, the president concludes the presentation with the appropriate prayer (CI: pp. 45, 43) before the candidates and their sponsors return to their places. On the Sunday when the Lord's Prayer has been presented, the Creed may be omitted so that the rite continues with the prayers of intercession. In some circumstances, it may be appropriate for catechesis on the text that has been presented to take place immediately, in which case the president may say to the candidates

Go in peace. May the Lord remain with you always

and they and their sponsors leave to meet as a group in an adjoining room, if there is one, or another suitable meeting place. (For further discussion of the Presentation of the Texts, see CI: pp. 328–9.)

Finally, a word needs to be said about those who have been members of a group such as Pilgrim and who have decided the time is not right for them to make a decision about being baptized, confirmed or affirming baptismal faith. It is important that the Call (or, indeed, the eventual celebration of the rites of initiation) doesn't ignore them, or make them feel in any way guilty about not progressing to this stage. The prayers can include thanksgiving for all those who have been members of the group and pray for them as well as for the others. In some cases, it may be appropriate for those who wish to continue the journey to be invited forward before the blessing and for prayer to be offered for them (see p. 32).

4

The baptism of infants and children

This chapter provides guidance for the baptism of infants as well as children who are able to answer for themselves. It has already been observed that, whereas the number of infant baptisms has been decreasing for some time, the number of children (5 to 12 years of age) being baptized increased by 15 per cent between 2004 and 2013 (p. xii). For the purposes of this guide, 'infants' will be used to refer to infants and children, unless the two categories of candidate need to be distinguished (for example, at the baptism itself), in which case both terms will be used.

When thinking afresh about how to celebrate the baptism of infants, in addition to deciding whether such baptisms should take place in a stand-alone rite or within the context of public worship (pp. xvii–xviii), and whether which, if any, of the ATAL should be used (p. xix) a number of other points require consideration. If a church has a font, it is nearly always best to use it rather than a bowl of water on a table (pp. 3–6). If the font is at the east end of the church, it may be possible to seat the congregation at the front of the nave or, with a small congregation, in a side chapel, and then move to the font, thus giving ritual expression to the notion of initiation as journey (CI: p. 9). The baptism of infants by immersion, though rarely performed in the Church of England, is perfectly possible, either in a font or a baptismal pool, and the latter is also appropriate to baptize children by immersion (see pp. 6, 62).

The importance of using a substantial quantity of water in baptism cannot be overemphasized (CI: p. 100, note 12). Water is the primary symbol of baptism. It needs to be used in such a way that it can be seen and heard by the whole congregation and, more importantly, experienced by candidates who are old enough as washing rather than being splashed or sprinkled. Symbolizing the generosity of God's grace, the drowning of sin and new life in the Spirit, whatever the design or position of the font, there is no excuse for the minimal use of water. In many cases it will be necessary to part-fill the font before the service and then top up to the brim with warmed water from a jug or ewer during the course of the rite. The vessel containing the water should be placed in full view of the congregation as they gather. If the removal of water from the font after the service is an issue, it may be necessary to place a bowl inside the font to hold the water. This should be appropriate for liturgical use (not a plastic washing-up bowl!), and large enough to hold a substantial quantity of water. And, of course, it goes without saying that the font and the water should be clean. A towel should be placed near the font, or on the edge of it, for drying the candidate's head and, if baptism is administered by immersion, the body as well. If the candidate is to be clothed after baptism, the baptismal garment will need to be left in a convenient place nearby. (For a more detailed discussion of the use of water in baptism and its associated symbolism, see ALG 4: pp. 23–34.)

The Easter Candle needs to be lit (see pp. 6–7), and candles for the candidates should be placed near it. At a stand-alone baptism in Eastertide, it may be best to move the Paschal Candle to the font for the whole service, or, if the first part of the rite takes place elsewhere, enlist the help of a member of the congregation or another member of the ministry team to carry it to the font at the appropriate moment. Although CW suggests that 'a large candle may be lit' immediately before the president introduces the Decision, 'In baptism, God calls us out of darkness into his marvellous light' (CI: p. 67), this may be introducing an unnecessary additional symbolic action to a rite that can easily become overloaded with symbols as well as with words.

As for the candidates' candles, these need to be of an appropriate size and design. Turrell describes them as 'small' (Turrell 2013: p. 98), but a three-inch candle from the pricket stand will not do! Research carried out for the Baptism Project reveals that, for the majority of parents, the giving of the candle is the most memorable and meaningful element of the baptism rite. Baptism candles are available in many different designs. Some of them have the advantage of looking like a small Easter Candle. Whatever its design, the family should be encouraged to take it home with them, and to light it on the anniversary of baptism, birthdays and other significant occasions.

Two oils may be used in the celebration of baptism: the oil of baptism (or catechumens) and the oil of chrism. The notes accompanying the baptism rite (CI: p. 100, note 10), the Liturgical Commission's commentary (CI: pp. 343, 345–6) and ATAL (pp. 5–6) provide guidance both on their symbolic meaning and how they may be used. The oil of baptism may be used at the Signing with the Cross after the Decision, and chrism at the anointing after baptism. TS explains that perfume or balsam (often referred to as the 'oil of flowers') is customarily added to the olive oil used for the chrism to give it a sweet smell (TS: p. 279, note 3). Enough needs to be added so that it can be clearly distinguished from the other two. If those responsible for preparing the oils for the Chrism Eucharist have not been sufficiently generous, it is possible to create a more pungent aroma by adding more perfume or balsam. In addition to being able to smell the chrism, the symbol can be much more vivid if both oils are also visible during the rite. To highlight their presence, they can be kept in glass cruets or jugs rather than being soaked into cotton wool or kept in small silver stocks, and placed on tables in a prominent position near to where they will be used. If substantial quantities of oil are used, it may be necessary to provide a lavabo to wash the president's hands when necessary.

The use of oil in baptism has a long history, and goes back to some of the earliest initiation rites for which there is evidence. It also resonates with the various ways in which oil is used in a number of contemporary cultures. Liturgically, it is not only 'part of the prayer which is integral to baptism' (CI: p. 345), but also gives visual expression to a number of important truths about the effects of the rite upon the newly baptized, which can be highlighted during the service. This is not to suggest that the president should explain what this and other symbols means (see pp. 1–2). The temptation to explain symbols is often great, particularly when ministering to a predominantly 'unchurched' congregation. Sometimes fed by a lack of confidence in their effectiveness, it can turn them into no more than a series of actions done to the candidate, rather than vivid God-given signs of transformative grace. There is a fine line between explaining what a symbol means, and highlighting it within the rite. It is not intended that no verbal reference should be made to anointing or any of the other symbolic actions; quite the opposite. One way to avoid killing a symbol through explanation is to resist telling the congregation what is going to happen and why immediately before the ritual is enacted. Thus the sermon, however brief and informal, provides an obvious opportunity to explore how, through baptism, the candidate becomes another 'anointed one', a Christ; another is the moment *after* the president has signed the candidate with the cross, and parents and godparents or sponsors are invited to do the same (CI: p. 100, note 11).

ALG 4 notes that one of the challenges of anointing after the Decision is that none of the texts associated with the Signing with the Cross make any explicit reference to oil or anointing, nor are the notes particularly illuminating in providing an explanation of why the candidate may be anointed at this point in the service (ALG 4: p. 46). That such an anointing reflects athletes preparing for a contest (CI: p. 100, note 10) may have a good patristic pedigree, being cited by St John Chrysostom (*c.* 309–407) and St Ambrose (337–397), but it provides little help to the minister who is thinking about how to perform it. By contrast, when it comes to the anointing with chrism after baptism the connection between the outpouring of God's grace and the anointing of his Spirit provides a helpful resonance with the liturgical action:

> May God . . . pour upon you the riches of his grace,
> . . . that . . . you may daily be renewed by his anointing Spirit.
>
> (CI: p. 89)

When both oils are used, if reference is made to anointing earlier in the service, the second anointing can more easily speak for itself. If it is preferred to use only one oil, the post-baptismal chrismation is the more significant of the two; the post-Decision signing can be performed without oil, if necessary.

Moving from the symbolic to the practical, careful thought needs to be given to what form any printed order of service will take. The Church of England publishes its own CW baptism cards, as does the Additional Curates Society (with some Roman additions; see <www.additionalcurates.co.uk>). Some parishes will produce their own cards, often laminated, which can be used on multiple occasions and, in others, a specially printed order of service will be used for each baptism. It is often tempting to print every word that the congregation will hear and say, not least since the president will be able to use the same text. However, this rarely enhances the congregation's active participation, and often has the opposite effect, giving them good reason not to look up to engage with the drama of the rite. As a general rule in this and any rite, it is best only to print the texts which the parents, godparents and congregation are required to say (including the Lord's Prayer). Texts such as the Collect, reading(s), and Prayer over the Water are not required. Whatever the design of the order of service, parishes may like to consider giving out the Baptism Project's Guest Bookmark, or a homemade equivalent, to accompany them, which people can be encouraged to take home. If a bespoke order of service has been produced, it should obviously include the name of the candidates and, with the consent of the parents, may include a photograph.

Finally, a decision needs to be made about whether it is appropriate to have a brief rehearsal with the parents and godparents, either immediately before the service or perhaps at another time, if they are able to attend. Although a separate rehearsal may not be possible in a number of contexts, where it is feasible, its purpose is not to drill participants in the hope that, on the day, they will not put a foot wrong, but to try to reduce any anxiety about what will happen during the service by showing them where they will stand and, if appropriate, practising some of the responses. When children are baptized, a rehearsal the day before may be particularly helpful. At the end of the rehearsal, it may be appropriate to say a prayer with the family, and to encourage them to light a candle at a statue or icon for those to be baptized.

Stand-alone baptism of infants

The advantages and disadvantages of a stand-alone rite have already been discussed (see pp. xvii–xviii). When baptism is celebrated outside the context of public worship, in addition to considering how the building and various symbols will be used, attention also needs to be paid to the structure of the rite: which elements within it are optional; where there is a choice of texts, which are most suitable; and at what points in the service the minister's own words may be preferred.

One frequently expressed frustration with CI is that so much material is provided that it is not always clear which rite to use on a particular occasion. The starting point here is the order for Baptism apart from a Celebration of Holy Communion (CI: pp. 80–95). It has the familiar CW shape with the Liturgy of Baptism being celebrated in response to the proclamation of God's word:

Table 4.1 Order for the stand-alone baptism of infants

		Mandatory	*Optional*
¶	Preparation		
		The Greeting	
			Introduction
		The Collect	
¶	The Liturgy of the Word		
			Reading(s)
			Gospel Acclamation
		Gospel reading	
		Sermon	
¶	The Liturgy of Baptism		
		Presentation of the Candidates	
		The Decision	
		The Signing with the Cross	
			Procession to the Font
		Prayer over the Water	
		Profession of Faith	
		Baptism	
		Commission	
			Prayers of Intercession
		Welcome and Peace	
¶	The Sending Out		
			The Blessing
			Giving of a Candle
		The Dismissal	

The Presentation of the Candidates can cause confusion. Although the act of presentation itself was made optional in 1999, the texts which follow it were not. If desired, the Presentation may take place between the Greeting and the Collect (CI: p. 98, note 4), and the candidate may be signed with the cross after baptism rather than following the Decision (CI: p. 100, note 11). The Commission may be deferred until the beginning of the Sending Out, if the newly baptized are able to answer for themselves; alternatively, it may be omitted, and its contents included in the sermon (CI: p. 101, note 15). The title 'Prayers of Intercession' is mistakenly printed as a major subheading (CI: p. 93), despite the fact that they are optional; if used, they may happen after, rather than before, the Welcome and Peace (CI: p. 101, note 16). The Giving of a Lighted Candle is also optional and, if used, may take place before the Dismissal or after the baptism.

A further point to be considered when preparing for a stand-alone baptism is whether one or two members of the congregation are able to be present to welcome people and, perhaps, assist at the service by reading, or holding the oil during the anointing, or in some other practical way. This may be a lay member of the ministry team, a baptism visitor, or anyone willing, by their presence, to enable a connection to be made with the local worshipping community. If baptism families subsequently return to a main Sunday service, perhaps responding to an invitation to come to an all-age liturgy at Easter, Christmas, Mothering Sunday or Harvest, these 'Baptism Buddies', as the Baptism Project refers to them (see <https://churchsupporthub. org/wp-content/uploads/2014/11/Making-families-welcome-in-template.pdf>), are well placed to welcome them, perhaps sitting with them during the service, and inviting them to refreshments afterwards.

Finally, consideration needs to be given to the optimal number of candidates to baptize in a stand-alone service. For practical and pastoral reasons, given the trend towards increasing numbers attending such services with, in some cases, the christening of a firstborn child taking the place of a wedding as *the* significant celebration for family and friends towards the beginning of a relationship, it may be best not to baptize more than two candidates (or children from two families) at a time. The size of the building will obviously be a determining factor. Pastorally, if one family group is much larger than the other, it is important that the candidates are treated equally and, if the parish has a 'Baptism Buddies' scheme, there should ideally be one for each family.

Preparation

The purpose of the Preparation is to use words of welcome to set up a relationship between the president and the people, to introduce the rite, and to open the service in prayer. This needs to be done as simply as possible, without overloading the opening rite with too many words. A stand-alone baptism will often begin informally once the congregation has gathered, preferably with parents and godparents sitting together with the candidate(s) at the front of the church. Given the informal nature of the gathering, it is sometimes a challenge to signal to the congregation that the service has begun. One way of doing this is for the president to robe (cotta, surplice or alb with white stole) once everyone is in place, and not to address the congregation as a whole until then. Standing in front of the congregation, if the president's first words are the Pauline greeting (CI: p. 81), such an opening will often fall flat, even if the dialogue is printed in an order of service. It is normally best to begin with informal words of welcome to attract people's attention and give a clear indication that the service is starting. Having begun in this way, a liturgical greeting is normally superfluous. If the context is such that a more formal opening is possible, the Greeting may be prefaced with the Trinitarian invocation, as at the Eucharist and, during Eastertide, followed by the Easter Acclamation. When 'In the name of the Father . . .' is used, 'The Lord be with you' may be preferred to a second Trinitarian formula.

As at the Eucharist, words of welcome and introduction may be combined (ALG 3: p. 32). The Ordinary Time and seasonal scripted introductions are densely packed with biblical imagery (CI: pp. 81, 150–65) and are often inappropriate at stand-alone celebrations where a simpler approach is desirable. Although any form of introduction is optional, it would be a mistake not to introduce the rite after the welcome, and perhaps highlight one biblical image or symbol which, like a thread, is going to be woven through the rite, holding the service together. CW makes provision for a prayer of thanksgiving to be used here (CI: p. 166). This may be particularly appropriate after a difficult birth.

The candidates may also be presented to the congregation during the Preparation (CI: p. 98, note 4). Although the presentation is optional, there is a need to introduce the candidates to the congregation at some point in the rite, and it may work best to do this informally as part of the welcome and introduction. If desired, a parent or godparent holding the infant may stand and face the congregation when the candidate's name is mentioned. Older children may be encouraged to stand with a parent or godparent and face the congregation.

The Preparation concludes with the Collect. At this point in the rite, it feels most natural to pray for the candidates to be baptized and their parents and godparents (particularly if the prayers later in the service are going to be omitted), yet the rubrics require the Collect of the Day or an alternative. The latter assumes that the congregation consists of those who have been baptized ('we who are born again') and, using the language of Ephesians 4.13, prays that they may grow into the 'full stature of Christ'. If such language sits uneasily with the context of the service, the president may take advantage of Canon B5.1 and, using his or her discretion, substitute the prayer of thanksgiving (CI: p. 166) for the Collect.

The Liturgy of the Word

At a stand-alone celebration, one reading, which, if there is only one reading, must be a passage from the Gospels, is likely to be sufficient. Where possible, it may be read by a family member, godparent or friend, or this may be an appropriate role for a 'Baptism Buddy' or assisting minister. Outside the context of the Eucharist, there is no requirement for people to stand while the Gospel is read, and, although not indicated as optional, the Gospel responses may be omitted (CI: p. 83). As for the choice of reading, CW encourages the use of the readings of the day on Sundays, Principal Feasts, other Principal Holy Days and Festivals (CI: p. 99, note 5). Whereas this will often be appropriate when baptism is celebrated at the principal Sunday service, it makes less sense to do so when it is not. Readings are provided for use in seasons and Ordinary Time (CI: pp. 150–65, 167). One of the accounts of the baptism of Jesus is an obvious choice, and links well with the use of oil and water later in the rite; so too, in Eastertide, one of the resurrection narratives, or a resurrection appearance, is often appropriate, and can be linked to the symbolism of the Easter Candle. If the alternative form of the Decision is used (ATAL: p. 35), the Parable of the Prodigal Son (Luke 15.11–end) or of the Lost Sheep (Luke 15.1–7) or Lost Coin (Luke 15.8–10) may be appropriate. Whichever reading is chosen, it is the responsibility of the president to think creatively about how it can be alluded to in different parts of the rite, such as the introduction mentioned above, as well as the sermon which follows it.

The sermon itself is likely to be relatively short and informal. If any children are present, they may be involved in an assembly-style question-and-answer dialogue with the preacher, and the use of a prop (such as the water, oil or a candle) may be appropriate. In churches that use screens, visual images or a short film may be part of the presentation. However it is delivered, the sermon provides an important opportunity to say something (perhaps no more than one thing) about baptism, and needs to be carefully prepared to provide appropriate content without the preacher being tied to a set of notes.

Note 15 (CI: p. 101) allows for the contents of the Commission to be included in the sermon. There are strong reasons why this is to be avoided, not least because it undermines the rite's theology of prevenient grace. Whereas the ASB's rite for the Baptism of Children required parents and godparents to assent to their duties before a child could be baptized, CW, following the BCP, has incorporated this within the post-baptismal commission. As Phillip Tovey and I have noted:

> This marks an important shift from the theological stance of the ASB and clearly states that divine grace is not dependent upon human initiative, but that the grace of God in baptism invites human response and responsibility. (CCW1: pp. 171–2)

For a more detailed discussion of this issue, and its relationship to the position of the Signing with the Cross, see my 'Outward Ceremony and Honourable Badge' (Jones 2010: p. 150).

The Liturgy of Baptism

Presentation of the Candidates

If it has not taken place already, the Liturgy of Baptism may begin with the Presentation of the Candidates (CI: p. 84). Although this is optional, each child needs to be introduced to the congregation at some point before the Decision. If the candidates include any children who are able to answer for themselves, the president may, after they have been presented, ask them if they wish to be baptized. For the Presentation, the congregation may be asked to stand, with parents, godparents and candidates facing them. The president needs to be positioned between them, perhaps slightly to one side, so that it's possible to turn to both baptism party and congregation at appropriate moments.

A choice has to be made about whether to use the default CW texts or ATAL. Given that, at a stand-alone baptism, there will often be few, if any, members of the local Christian community present, the first of the original questions, in which the congregation is addressed as the 'People of God', sometimes causes confusion as to who is being referred to, and the allusion to Acts 2.47 in 'In baptism the Lord is adding to our number those whom he is calling' introduces an unwelcome degree of theological complexity which is not easily understood.

That said, the emphasis on divine initiative (faith being God's gift, and baptism being a response to God's call) is welcome and needs to be expressed liturgically. The first of the alternative texts achieves this with its opening quotation from Mark 10.14, 'Let the little children come to me', and its subsequent reference to Christ welcoming the candidates into his Church. The congregation, no longer referred to as the 'people of God', is asked two simple questions: if they will support the candidates as they begin their journey of faith, and if they will help them live and grow within God's family. Turning then to the parents and godparents, the president draws on Isaiah 43.1 to assert that God knows every person by name, and that all people belong to him (a theme which will be reinforced at the Signing with the Cross), before asking the parents and godparents if they will pray for the candidates and help them to follow Christ. This question also makes clear that those answering are not speaking for themselves but for the candidates: 'You speak for *these children* today.' Referred to as proxy speaking or proxy faith, the parents and godparents act as the child's mouthpiece. This is an important theological principle in both BCP 1662 and CW, and reflects patristic practice. (For more on this, see CI: pp. 340–2; CCW1: pp. 164–5.)

The Decision

Having established the divine initiative in baptism, Christ's welcome, and the support of parents, godparents and congregation, there now follows the candidate's decision to reject evil and turn to Christ. This corresponds to the *apotaxis* (renunciation) and *syntaxis* (adherence) in the early Eastern tradition, in which it was one of the most dramatic parts of the adult rite. The liturgy in fourth-century Jerusalem, described by St Cyril, required the candidate to face west for the renunciation and east for the adherence, symbolizing the candidate's radical change of allegiance from Satan to Christ. Likewise, in one of the baptismal homilies of St John Chrysostom, the candidate is made to kneel, adopting 'the posture of captivity':

> The priests who introduce you first of all tell you to kneel down and pray with your hands raised to heaven, and by this attitude of body recall to your mind the one from whom you have been delivered and the other whom you are about to join.
>
> (*Baptismal Homily* 2.18; Yarnold 1994: p. 158)

This powerful act of deliverance from Satan and being joined to Christ is one with which the contemporary Church struggles. The lack of accessible language in the Decision, highlighted by the Diocese of Liverpool's motion to General Synod in 2011 (GS 1816A), is only part of the problem; equally problematic is the widespread mis-understanding about the identity of the devil who, in the popular imagination, is depicted as a trident-bearing scarlet, menacing figure with horns and hooves. At this point in the rite, through text and the way in which it is performed, something of the 'awe-inspiring' drama of the fourth-century rite needs to be experienced. This is, of course, easier said than done, but it presents a challenge which should not be shied away from.

In terms of text, there are now three options: the default CW version (CI: p. 85), the ASB text (CI: p. 168), and ATAL (ATAL: p. 35). In the logic of the rite, turning to Christ follows the renunciation of evil. That being the case, however strong the 'pastoral reasons' for using the ASB text (CW is silent on what these pastoral reasons might be), its use runs counter to the dramatic flow of renunciation, adherence and signing. Having renounced evil and turned to Christ, the candidate's belonging to Christ is given ritual expression in the signing. Thus the Decision sets up a new personal relationship with Christ who, in response to the transfer of allegiance that has taken place, claims the candidate for his own.

The default CW version is cast in the form of two sets of three questions, addressed to infants through their parents and godparents. In addition to what has already been said about the devil, the overall linguistic register of the dialogue, the appropriateness of the language of submission, and the preamble's use of two strong biblical images (1 Peter 2.9; Romans 6.8) within the space of two sentences has undoubtedly, and understandably, led many clergy to prefer the ASB version in a stand-alone context. But this is no longer the only refuge of clergy who want to reject 'the devil and all rebellion against God'!

ATAL consists of four questions, to which the answer to each is a simple 'I do'. The introduction asserts the divine initiative in salvation, drawing on the Parable of the Prodigal Son. It is inclusive in its reference to sin ('We all wander far from God and lose our way'), identifies Christ as the one who 'comes to find us and welcomes us home', and baptism as the means by which human beings can respond to the call home. The questions that follow are much simpler than the default text. Their simplicity gives them a sharper focus and greater power. The response to Christ's call in baptism requires a turning away from sin and a rejection of evil in order to turn to Christ as Saviour and trust in him as Lord. A rubric between the two sets of questions suggests that this turning can be ritualized by inviting the candidates, parents and godparents to turn physically at this point. The accompanying notes give some suggestions as to how this might be done:

> The first pair of questions might typically be answered facing away from the east, and the second pair after turning to face a symbolic location of new life in the risen Christ, such as the font, holy table or Easter Candle. (ATAL: p. 5)

For such a turning to be an effective symbol, the baptism family needs to be warned that it will happen (it is something that can be discussed as part of the baptism preparation), and it may be helpful to rehearse it briefly before the service. A rubric in the order of service reminding them to do it may help, as well as a 'Baptism Buddy' standing with them to give a lead. Whatever happens, the president should resist the temptation to disempower the symbol by explaining what is about to happen just before the moment comes. To be effective, it needs to speak for itself. It is also important, as the notes suggest, to think about where the president should stand at this point, so that it doesn't appear that the group is turning towards him or her. Although St Cyril would have the candidates turn from west ('the quarter from which darkness appears to us') to east ('the region of light'), this may cause confusion in many church buildings if it means that the group will turn their backs on the congregation after the renunciation, remain with their backs turned for the consignation, and then turn towards darkness again when all move to the font! Although a decision on how this is best performed will depend on the layout of the building, in some churches it may work for the group to stand with their backs to the congregation as the Decision is introduced ('We all wander far from God and lose our way'), and then turn to face them, and the font, if it is at the west end, for the adherence. The default CW text can be performed with the same movement between the two sets of questions. ATAL is particularly appropriate for children who are able to answer for themselves.

Signing with the Cross

The Decision is followed immediately by the Signing with the Cross. Although this may be postponed until after baptism (mirroring its position in BCP 1662), to do so interrupts the dramatic flow of the rite and undermines its theology of prevenient grace, since the formula 'Christ claims you as his own' (CI: p. 86) can only be used when the consignation takes place before baptism (CI: p. 100, note 11; for further discussion of this, see my 'Outward Ceremony and Honourable Badge', Jones 2010: pp. 151–2). Structurally and theologically, this anointing with the oil of baptism symbolizes God's invitation to salvation, the candidates' acceptance of the same once-for-all act of God in Christ, and the Anointed One claiming them as his anointed children by marking them with his sign, the sign from which flows the grace by which the candidates will be able to 'remain faithful to Christ'. All of this makes perfect theological and liturgical sense but, as has already been mentioned (p. 45), the president is not helped by being confronted with a series of texts that make no reference to oil. (For further discussion of this, and how the Church of England's baptism rite has combined consignation and anointing, two separate liturgical acts in the catechumenal process, see ALG 4: pp. 46–7.)

When it comes to the signing, if the oil is kept in a glass jug or cruet, it may be poured, in full view of the congregation, by a 'Baptism Buddy', godparent or another minister, into the palm of the president's hand, or into a shallow bowl, and taken from there to sign the candidate's forehead. If there are several candidates and/or sponsors, pouring a larger amount into a bowl may be more practical. As a general rule, whenever oil is used, it is more important to be concerned about making the anointing a visible and generous symbol than about making a mess.

Significantly, no alternative to the CW formula, 'Christ claims you for his own. Receive the sign of his cross', has been provided in ATAL. The CW formula says everything that is required at this point in the rite, and is short and simple enough to be memorized so that the president can say it while making the signing of the cross, normally with the right thumb, on the child's forehead. Having addressed the infant through parents and godparents in the Decision, when it comes to the signing, the president needs to address the candidate directly.

To make it obvious that this is happening, he or she can be addressed by name at the beginning of the formula.

CW permits the president to delegate the signing to another minister (CI: p. 86; p. 100, note 11). This seems unnecessary, particularly since others are permitted to sign the candidate with the cross after the initial signing has taken place. Although CW restricts those invited to do this to parents, godparents and sponsors, it would seem appropriate to include any ordained or lay minsters present who have been involved in baptism preparation, as well as a 'Baptism Buddy', if there is one.

If the signing is likely to take some time, and someone other than the president is able to hold the oil, the president can use the opportunity to say something about the significance of the signing (see pp. 44–5). Once all the candidates have been signed, the president addresses them again (as a group), using the form in CI, page 68, or ATAL, page 36. The latter removes the militaristic language of the original ('Stand bravely' in place of 'Fight valiantly') and also replaces 'against sin, the world and the devil' with 'against all the powers of evil'. As this will be the first time that the congregation has had to respond collectively since the Presentation, a prompt to look at the order of service may be necessary. The final prayer begins with a petition for deliverance, and expresses the belief that the image of God's glory, in which the candidates were created, will be restored to them as a result of their identification with the Second Adam, who will lead them from darkness to light. The additional text is simply an abbreviated version of the original version, removing the second line. Although it is suggested that 'where one of the alternative sections is used, that section should be used in its entirety: existing and additional provision should not be combined within a given section' (ATAL: p. 3), no harm will be done if the full version of the final prayer is used here. As it is said, the president's right hand may be laid on the head of each of the candidates; alternatively, both hands may be extended, palms down, over the candidates. The prayer is said only once. If it is possible to memorize it, the president's attention can be focused on the candidates and the ritual action.

Prayer over the Water

If the opening part of the rite has taken place in the nave or a side chapel, the president and baptismal party now need to gather at the font. This need not be just a practical necessity. The movement that is required can be used to illustrate the concept of journey: journey with Christ to the waters of baptism, or the Christian life itself as a journey that begins with baptism. If possible, the whole congregation should gather round the font, with the children at the front so that what is happening is visible to them and they can be involved. During Eastertide, someone can be asked to carry the Easter Candle (see p. 43); one of the godparents can be given the jug or ewer containing the water; and, if the parish has an icon of the baptism of Jesus, this can be given to a child to carry and placed next to the font, to make a link between Jesus' baptism and that of the candidate. Although CW suggests that 'A canticle, psalm, hymn, or litany may be used' (CI: p. 87), this may be inappropriate at a stand-alone celebration, and a more informal procession to the font, led by the president and the baptismal party, or the Easter Candle, may be more suitable. However, if the service is to include a hymn, perhaps one requested by the family, it is probably best sung now.

Once all have gathered, water is poured into the font in such a way that can be seen and heard by the congregation. There need be no concern about making a splash (although slippery stone steps can present a safety hazard)! Where possible, a godparent should be encouraged to pour the water (ATAL: p. 6). (For further discussion on the use of water, see pp. 42–3 and ALG 4: pp. 25–34.)

Since the Prayer over the Water is central to the rite, the baptismal equivalent of the Eucharistic Prayer, it is unsurprising that, historically, it is often a very lengthy text. The CW Ordinary Time and seasonal versions (CI: pp. 87, 150–65) have been criticized both for their length and for the biblical literacy required to understand them. As Tim Stratford noted in the 2011 paper which accompanied the Diocese of Liverpool motion to General Synod:

> All four (prayers) were felt to depend heavily on an understanding of salvation history that is not possessed by most baptism congregations in high IMD (Index of Multiple Deprivation) parishes ... There was a strong plea from among the high IMD clergy for a shorter prayer in direct but poetic language that allows the gospel to resonate better with people's experience of life.   (GS 1816A: p. 3)

The Liturgical Commission has sought to achieve this by offering two much shorter prayers, one combining Exodus typology with

Romans 6, the other based on the Jordan event. If either of these texts is used, there is no opening dialogue between the president and people. The responsive forms of the four original CW texts were devised to encourage greater congregational participation, but their disadvantage is that one of them requires the full text to be printed in the order of service (CI: p. 153) and in the others the repeated response needs to be memorized if the congregation is to be encouraged to lift their heads from the order of service. Whichever text is used, it must be performed well if it is to engage people and hold their attention. If the president's copy can be held by an assistant or rest easily on the side of the font, the president's hands should be kept together for the opening responses (if any) and then held in the *orans* position until the Spirit is invoked upon, or God is asked to bless, the water. At that point the president may spread the hands, slightly overlapping with palms facing down, over the water, and may then make the sign of the cross in the water with the right hand, as in a eucharistic epiclesis. For example:

> Now sanctify this water that,
> *(hands spread palms down)* by the power of your Holy Spirit,
> they may be *(make sign of the cross in the water)* cleansed from sin
>   and born again. (CI: p. 87)

or:

> Now send *(hands spread palms down)* your Spirit,
> that those who are washed in this water
> may die with Christ *(make sign of the cross in the water)* and rise
>   with him. (ATAL: p. 37)

The hands are then held in the *orans* position until the end of the prayer when they are brought together for the final doxology, and the people respond with their Amen (the cue may need to be printed in the order of service). (For further guidance on manual acts, see ALG 3: pp. 3–4, 66–7.)

Profession of Faith

The Apostles' Creed has its origins as a baptismal profession of faith. Indeed, in some early traditions, the credal interrogations took place while the candidate stood in the water and were, in effect, the baptismal formula (see CCW1: p. 169). But whose faith is being professed here? In BCP 1662, the godparents express the faith of the child ('Dost thou, in the name of this Child ... ?'). In ASB, the parents and godparents answered for themselves and for the child (ASB: p. 247). In CW, unlike the Decision which, as we have seen, has returned to proxy speaking, the faith that is professed is the faith of the Church. This is not, as the Liturgical Commission's commentary makes clear, 'a test for the candidate', whatever their age:

> Candidates are asked to join in a congregational recitation rather than making such a full statement on their own, thereby demonstrating that they are joining, and being drawn into, a community of faith.
>
> (CI: p. 334)

That said, since the president's introduction invites the congregation to profess 'together with *these candidates* the faith of the Church' (CI: p. 88), there is a sense in which the parents and godparents are articulating the Church's faith on behalf of the candidates as well as themselves.

Here there is a choice between using an interrogatory form of the Apostles' Creed (a slightly amended form of the ecumenically agreed *English Language Liturgical Consultation* text; for further details, see CI: p. 335) or, 'where there are strong pastoral reasons', the much briefer question and answer form (CI: p. 178), which is very similar to that which appeared in the ASB, amended in response to criticism that the ASB form divided 'the work of creation, redemption and sanctification among the separate persons of the Trinity in a way that could be conceived as modalist' (CI: p. 335). Although, arguably, the CW version still has a whiff of modalism about it, it is not for this reason that the commentary expresses concern about its use:

> The caution in the rubric ... arises from a respect for the Anglican position that the Apostles' Creed is 'the baptismal symbol' or profession (Lambeth Quadrilateral, 1888). It is also important to avoid any impression of 'first' and 'second' class baptism, or any suggestion that some baptisms require a greater degree of commitment than others.
>
> (CI: p. 334)

Furthermore, the commentary goes on to say that any decision about which profession to use is not simply a matter of the Apostles' Creed being more suited to adults, and the shorter form to children (CI: p. 335). All of this is undoubtedly true. And yet, in many situations where baptism is being celebrated apart from public worship, a long and theologically complex congregational text at this point in the rite presents a challenge which is not easily overcome. Indeed, unlike the equally lengthy Prayer over the Water, since most of the profession text is congregational, there is little opportunity to help people engage with it by the way in which it is performed. By careful timing of the questions, the president can try to keep the momentum going, but it is not easy to prevent the rite from slowing down, or even grinding to a halt, just before the centre-point of baptism is reached. If, for these reasons, the alternative form is used, it may be preferable to replace its introduction with the form on page 88 of this book, emphasizing that what is being expressed is 'the faith of the Church'. When children able to answer for themselves are being baptized, the alternative form is likely to be preferred.

Baptism

The rite reaches its climax as the candidates are baptized. If they include any children who are able to speak for themselves, they may be asked whether the profession of faith that has just been made is also their faith.

When infants are baptized, although BCP 1662 prefaces the baptism with the priest asking the godparents to name the child, there is no CW equivalent, and nor should there be. In the Prayer Book rite, the rubrics require the child to be baptized no later than 'the first or second Sunday next after their birth', thus making the connection between birth and baptism much stronger, with the latter providing a convenient opportunity for the child to be named publically. In today's context, birth and baptism are rarely in such close proximity; the naming will have taken place sometime before, and been legally ratified when the birth was registered. Although it is possible to add a baptismal forename to a child whose birth was registered within the previous 12 months (for guidance on this, see the *Guidebook for the Clergy* issued by the General Register Office), it is important to remember that, theologically, baptism is not a naming ceremony. If the president is concerned about remembering the name of the child, a sticky note is always a better option than to invite the parents to 'Name this child'!

CW permits a minister other than the president to administer baptism (CI: p. 100, note 12). If there is a strong pastoral connection between the candidate's family and the other minister, this may be appropriate. Equally, if the baptism takes place at the Parish Eucharist, and the minister who has been involved in baptism preparation is not the president of the rite (see p. 10), an exception may be made. However, in the majority of cases, to delegate baptism to another minister runs the risk of signalling that it is less important than other parts of the rite, and is therefore to be avoided.

As to the method of baptism, CW, following BCP 1662, permits dipping or pouring (immersion or affusion):

> A threefold administration of water (whether by dipping or pouring) is a very ancient practice of the Church and is commended as testifying to the faith of the Trinity in which candidates are baptized. Nevertheless, a single administration is also lawful and valid.
>
> (CI: p. 100, note 12)

Unless there are strong pastoral reasons for water to be poured only once, a threefold administration is always to be preferred. For infants, if they are baptized by affusion, they may be held over the font by a parent, godparent or by the minister. If a 'substantial amount of water' is to be used (CI: p. 100, note 12), thought needs to be given to how it should be administered. A cupped hand, or a baptismal shell, however beautiful, will often not produce the desired effect. While being careful to pour the water over the baby's head, avoiding its eyes, nose and mouth, the best option may be to fill a medium-sized jug with water from the font, and pour water from it while saying the formula. As this can be a messy business, and the baptismal formula is easily memorized, it's often best to put the president's book to one side, or give it to someone to hold. If the anointing with chrism follows immediately, with the baby still held over the font, the president says the post-baptismal prayer (CI: p. 89) and pours chrism over the crown of the head at the line 'pour upon you the riches of his grace'. The commentary suggests that, to distinguish this anointing from that at the Decision, the chrism may be applied in the shape of a chi-rho, signifying *Christos*, the Anointed One (p. 336). This unprecedented action seems to over-complicate the symbol unnecessarily, and prevent it from speaking for itself. Far simpler and more powerful would be to reflect Old Testament practice and, using a larger quantity of oil than at the Decision, pour chrism over the crown of the head – thus making a bold and vivid gesture which can be easily seen and smelt.

Again, if it is possible for the president to memorize this text, that would be desirable. The anointing complete, the president, parent or godparent may use a towel to dry the head, removing any excess water or oil. In many communities it is now rare for a child to be clothed during the baptismal rite. If a family christening gown is used, the child often arrives wearing it. However, if the child is to be clothed during the service, it would be best for this to happen now, rather than before the anointing. Once this has been done, the president may address the candidate with the formula provided, 'linking practical necessity with scriptural imagery' (CI: p. 101, note 14; Galatians 3.27 and Colossians 3.10), before continuing with the service.

If infants are to be baptized by immersion, their clothes will need to be removed after the profession of faith. While this is happening, the president can roll up his or her sleeves (in this case, a cassock-alb is the most convenient garment to wear). Turrell gives helpful advice on how to baptize an infant by immersion:

> The infant is taken in the crook of the arm by the minister and then lowered into the font three times, taking care not to immerse the nose and mouth, while the minister says the baptismal formula. The candidate is given back to the parents and godparents, who are also given a towel by a server. (Turrell 2013: p. 93)

When thinking about when best to chrismate the candidate, it may depend on how the child reacts to the immersion! One possibility would be for the president to continue to hold the child in one arm, and anoint with chrism immediately after the baptism (as described above). Alternatively, if it seems best to return the child to a parent after the baptism, chrismation can follow once the candidate has been wrapped in a towel, and is being held by a parent. After the anointing, the infant can be dried and clothed.

When the candidates include older children (i.e. not babes in arms), the exact method of baptism will vary depending on whether they are able to stand at the font (perhaps on a box) and lean over or, for younger children, are best seated on the edge of the font, held by a parent or godparent, and tilted backwards when the water and oil are poured over the head. If they are baptized by immersion, the guidance in the next chapter should be followed, and a parent or godparent should accompany the child into the water and help them to dry and change afterwards.

The final rubric on page 89 of CI suggests that 'the president and those who have been baptized may return from the font'. This innocuous rubric highlights a problem which many clergy experience with the CW baptism rite when used apart from public worship: that is, how to maintain a sense of momentum, and engagement with the congregation, once the candidates have been baptized. Up until this point, everything that has been said and done has pointed towards the font. What now? The rite may stall if the congregation returns to where the service started. As previously suggested (pp. 8–9), to emphasize the link between baptism and Eucharist within the process of initiation, the Easter Candle could lead the congregation from the font to the altar for the prayers and the Sending Out. Alternatively, it may be best to remain standing round the font for the rest of the rite.

Commission

The additional texts have helped to clarify the purpose of the Commission. Addressed to the congregation, parents and godparents, it should include:

- the welcome of the Church, local and universal;
- the importance of belonging to the Christian community;
- the responsibilities of parents and godparents;
- the challenge to grow in Christian discipleship (ATAL: p. 38).

CW permits the Commission to be delegated to another minister, but this should normally be seen as exceptional, with the same principles applying as for the baptism itself.

Wherever possible, the president should try to 'talk directly and simply in his or her own words to the parents, godparents and congregation . . . covering the topics listed in the bullet points'. This is not necessarily an easy task, but is nearly always better than 'giving the impression that a written text is simply being read out' (ATAL: p. 7). ATAL provides examples of what this might sound like, using a register of language which is very different from CI. Although there may be a temptation simply to read one of these, ministers are being encouraged to craft their own, in language which is appropriate to their situation and context. The Commission need not, indeed, should not, be very long. Initially, at least, it may be helpful for some notes, or bullet points, to be used as an aide-memoire, and it may be helpful for the Commission to refer back to the reading, one of the symbols that has been highlighted during the course of the service, or a point that was made in the sermon.

Another set of bullet points is provided to structure the Commission when the newly baptized are able to answer for themselves and the Commission is addressed to them (ATAL: p. 38). One text from the original provision which has found favour in some quarters is the address to the newly baptized which begins, 'N and N, today God has touched you with his love' (CI: p. 91). Although it does not cover all of the bullet points, if it works well in a particular context, it may be a useful option if the president feels that a scripted form of words is essential.

Prayers of Intercession

The intercessions are optional, but it seems natural to want to pray for the candidates, parents and godparents. Moreover, although more relevant for adult candidates rather than children, it is nevertheless the case that the 'prayers draw the newly baptized into the praying Church of which they are now part' (CI: p. 101, note 16). CW makes provision for the intercessions to be placed before or after the Welcome and Peace. The suggestion here is that the eucharistic structure be maintained, and they should follow the Commission, which can end with an invitation to pray. Whether a set form is used (a congregational response is best avoided at a stand-alone celebration), or the president continues in his or her own words, they should conclude with the Lord's Prayer, for which the president's hands may be held in the *orans* position, as at the Eucharist (ALG 3: p. 72). Structuring the rite in this way allows the Welcome and Peace to move naturally into the Sending Out.

The Welcome and Peace

Within the logic and dramatic flow of the rite, the reality of incorporation into the life of the Church, universal and local, through baptism is expressed liturgically as the candidate is welcomed and the Peace shared. At a stand-alone celebration, this is another element that can cause difficulty if no, or very few, members of the church community are present to do the welcoming. In some places, this has led to the Welcome (and also, sometimes, the Giving of the Lighted Candle) being deferred until a Sunday morning service, perhaps most appropriately an all-age service, to which those recently baptized are invited to attend with their families, and the Welcome takes place before the Peace, or at the Dismissal if the candle is given at the same time, and it's necessary to process to the font to light it. ATAL provides some official sanction for such a welcome, though it is silent on whether this is in addition to, or in place of, that in the rite itself:

> Where a baptism has taken place at a separate service, the family may be invited to return at a principal service for the child to be welcomed by the wider congregation. (ATAL: p. 8)

Whenever, and however many times, the Welcome takes place, it is appropriate for the congregation to have an opportunity to welcome the candidate with applause, and this can lead naturally into the Peace, after which people may greet the newly baptized and each other. Even at a stand-alone baptism, it soon becomes obvious what to do at this point in the service.

The Sending Out

The final part of the rite consists of three elements: the Blessing, Giving of a Lighted Candle, and Dismissal (CI: p. 77), the first two of which are optional. Although the suggested order has a liturgical logic to it, to separate blessing and dismissal does not always feel comfortable, particularly at a stand-alone celebration of infant baptism. There may, therefore, be an argument for giving the candle first, and then blessing and dismissing the congregation. It is also possible to move the giving of the candle to its post-baptismal ASB position (CI: p. 101, note 17), so that it is connected more obviously to the baptism itself. If the earlier position is preferred, the candle would be most appropriately given immediately after the anointing with chrism. The practical problem with the earlier position is that it is sometimes difficult to know what to do with the candle once it has been lit, and to keep it alight for the remainder of the service. A positive reason for giving the candle at the end of the rite is expressed by the Liturgical Commission's commentary:

> The text . . . indicates that the primary symbolism is an apostolic summons to shine in the world, which is appropriate to the Sending out of the whole people of God. (CI: p. 338)

Whenever the candle is given, it should be lit from the Easter Candle, which may need to have been carried from the font to the place where the rite concludes (see p. 8). If there are several candidates, a 'Baptism

Buddy' may assist in giving them to godparents, parents or children who are old enough to receive the candle themselves. The formula is said only once, when all the candles have been given.

The theological language used in the blessing and its seasonal alternatives may feel overly complex at a stand-alone celebration. One possibility would be to omit the first part of the text altogether, and begin with 'The blessing of God almighty . . .'. If a longer text is preferred, the Aaronic blessing (NPFW: p. 302) or the following may be suitable:

> The love of the Lord Jesus
> draw you to himself,
> the power of the Lord Jesus
> strengthen you in his service,
> the joy of the Lord Jesus fill your hearts;
> and the blessing . . .   (NPFW: p. 302)

The president makes the sign of the cross over the people as the blessing is given (ALG 3: pp. 2 and 77). If the president is a deacon, the *us* form is used, and the sign of the cross is made over the body. Although it may be introduced by the greeting, 'The Lord be with you' and its response, if a further dialogue at this stage in the rite is considered to be liturgical overload, it may be omitted, particularly since the dismissal which follows is of greater significance. The president's hands remained joined as the dismissal is given, and 'Alleluia, alleluia' may be added to versicle and response during Eastertide.

A stand-alone rite will often end informally. It may be more appropriate for the president to stay with the family to give out any baptism certificates and cards to parents and godparents, as well as the box for the candle, if there is one, rather than disappearing to the sacristy. The end of the rite is also an opportunity for photographs to be taken, for which the family may want to regroup at the font. Although it is becoming increasingly difficult to discourage photography and filming during the service itself, any such plea can sometimes be more persuasive with the promise of a photo shoot at the end.

Infant baptism at the Sunday Eucharist

The baptism of infants at the Sunday Eucharist presents many opportunities. It allows the Christian community to support the candidates in prayer and be reminded of their own baptismal vocation and identity.

It also enables the baptismal party to worship with the Christian community (perhaps for the first time) and to experience baptism *and* Eucharist as sacraments of initiation. Nevertheless, the incorporation of the baptismal rite into the Sunday liturgy also presents its own challenges. This may involve a careful balancing act so that, for the usual congregation, the liturgy bears a sufficiently strong family likeness to the normal pattern of Sunday worship so that they are 'at home' with it, and, for those who are visiting, it is sufficiently accessible.

Accessibility is not something that the liturgy has to bear on its own. Consideration also needs to be given to how and by whom the baptismal parties are made welcome (both when they arrive and after the service has finished), where they are seated, and what books or booklets are given to them to enable them to participate. If it is possible to have a 'Baptism Buddy' for each family (see p. 48), a light touch is needed so that the family doesn't feel smothered. Wherever possible, the Buddy should have met the family before the service (either by being part of any preparation, or visiting them at home), and meet with them again afterwards, even if only to drop off a card, or to invite them to church on an appropriate occasion. At the baptism itself, they can be waiting for the family when they arrive, sit with them (towards the front of the nave, but probably not making them feel exposed in the front row), guide them through the service and, if the family is able to stay for refreshments afterwards, introduce them to some other members of the congregation. Ideally, the president should also welcome the family before the service begins and, unless having to take another service immediately afterwards, spend time with them at the end. The Baptism Project makes a number of simple, practical suggestions of how to enable the local community to welcome, and celebrate with, a baptism family (see <https://church-supporthub.org/wp-content/uploads/2014/11/10-or-more-things-to-do-at-your-next-baptism.pdf>). In addition, providing a christening cake, cupcakes or some other sort of celebratory refreshment after the service is a good way of expressing the church's support.

As for the order of service, if resources allow, the best option is to produce a one-off booklet which contains all the texts the congregation will need, including the hymns or songs and, with the permission of parents, photos of the candidates. If this can be done, special versions for parents and godparents can be provided in which the texts which they will say on their own are highlighted. If it is not possible or practical to produce a new booklet every time baptism is celebrated at the Sunday Eucharist, another option is to have a booklet which can be used repeatedly on such occasions, which can be given out with a hymn book or leaflet. The general principle to be followed here is to give out as few books and pieces of paper as possible.

The structure of the rite can be found on page 60 of CI, and CW provides additional guidance on how baptism may be celebrated at the Sunday Eucharist (CI: pp. 78–9). Once again, in planning the service, it's important to have a clear understanding of shape, and also which parts are mandatory and which optional. Much of what has already been said about stand-alone baptisms is relevant in this context (see pp. 46–66), and should be read alongside the guidance provided here. The following table provides an outline of what a celebration of baptism in the context of the Eucharist might look like:

Table 4.2 Order for infant baptism at the Sunday Eucharist

		Mandatory	*Optional*
¶	Preparation		
			Entrance Hymn
		The Greeting	
			Introduction
			Gloria in excelsis
		The Collect	
¶	The Liturgy of the Word		
			Reading(s)
			Gospel Acclamation
		Gospel reading	
		Sermon	
¶	The Liturgy of Baptism		
		Presentation of the Candidates	
		The Decision	
		The Signing with the Cross	
			Procession to the Font
		Prayer over the Water	
		Profession of Faith	
		Baptism	
		Commission	
			Prayers of Intercession
		Welcome and Peace	

Table 4.2 (*cont'd*)

	Mandatory	Optional
¶ The Liturgy of the Eucharist		
		Offertory Hymn
	Preparation of the Table	
	Taking of the Bread and Wine	
	The Eucharistic Prayer	
	The Lord's Prayer	
	Breaking of the Bread	
	Giving of Communion	
	Prayer after Communion	
¶ The Sending Out		
		Final hymn
		The Blessing
		Giving of a Candle
	The Dismissal	

Although it is obviously important that there is a family resemblance between this rite and what normally happens on a Sunday morning, it is important to remember that this service should not be presented as the Sunday Eucharist into which the baptism rite has been carefully squeezed in order to cause as little disruption as possible, nor is it a baptism service targeted at visitors, to which the Eucharist is tacked on the end to appease those regular members of the congregation who want to make their Sunday communion. It is, rather, an integrated celebration of the two sacraments of initiation, baptism and the Eucharist, and it is the task of the president to ensure that this is articulated through its celebration. If, as will normally be the case, the newly baptized are not going to receive communion after their baptism, and likewise their parents, godparents, family and friends, this can be a challenge. But it should not tempt the local community into turning the celebration of baptism at a principal Sunday service into a non-eucharistic rite. Having succeeded in introducing communion before confirmation, the logical next step is for infant communion to be put on the Church of England's agenda. This is something that clergy may want to discuss with colleagues at clergy chapter, with a view to raising it at deanery or diocesan synod. Although, as has already been discussed, the Church of England's view on whether baptism constitutes full sacramental initiation is confused (see pp. xiii–xvi), Turrell argues persuasively for the theological and pastoral logic of infant communion:

> [T]he reception of communion . . . completes the initiatory process . . .
> *all* neophytes need to receive communion, not just adults and older
> children. Not to communicate infants and younger children at their
> own baptisms is to delay their participation in the life of the body into
> which they have just been initiated and it puts the lie to all of our
> theological statements about baptism being full initiation.
>
> (Turrell 2013: pp. 100–1)

All that said, and despite the recommendation by IALC's 1985 Boston Statement, reiterated in the 1991 Toronto Statement, that 'all who are baptized should be welcomed into the eucharistic fellowship of the church' (Holeton 1993: pp. 254, 232), we should be under no illusion as to how long it may take for infant communion to be sanctioned by General Synod! Nevertheless, if the normal pattern of worship in a local church is eucharistic, the community has a responsibility to be itself in presenting its ecclesial identity to visitors, a responsibility that can be used as an opportunity to be confident that its liturgy is its most powerful tool for mission. This is a much more positive and honest approach than feeling the need to apologize for what normally happens on a Sunday, or for the community to treat the Eucharist as a service for insiders rather than, together with baptism, the life-changing drama of salvation in which all are invited to play a part. (For a discussion on the effects of infant communion, see G. Kerr-Wilson and T. Perkins, 'Consequences of Infant Communion' in Holeton 1993: pp. 63–71; and for a detailed historical account, see Mark Dalby's (2003, 2009) two-volume work.)

So what will the celebration of infant baptism at the Sunday Eucharist look like? This will depend, in part, on how frequently baptism is administered on a Sunday morning. A monthly baptismal liturgy may look quite different from one that is used once or twice a year. In parishes where this is a frequent occurrence, it may be possible to identify particular Sundays for the celebration of baptism (among them Easter and Pentecost), and to avoid others (including Lent). Another factor may be whether the baptism party contains members of the usual congregation, or whether it consists mainly of visitors. Yet another may be whether the community has a regular 'all-age Eucharist' which differs in style and content from that on other Sundays. The former may well be the best starting point for a celebration of baptism within the Sunday Eucharist and, indeed, there is much to be said for this being a Sunday when children are encouraged to be present for the whole service. While the style of celebration will undoubtedly vary from place to place, it is important never to give the impression that one celebration of Christian initiation is in any way superior to another; and, likewise, that baptism celebrated within the context of the Eucharist is superior to that which takes place outside it.

Preparation

The liturgy begins in the usual way. Whether or not it is decided to follow the parish's own all-age model, in choosing the music for the service, it may help visitors acclimatize to the building and the liturgy if at least some of the music is familiar to them, the entrance hymn being a particular case in point. The Greeting may be that normally used on a Sunday, rather than the form given on page 63 of CI, and this can be followed by an unscripted welcome and introduction (see pp. 48–9), leading into the *Gloria in excelsis*, when it is appointed. To avoid having to announce the Gloria, a cue is often helpful, which can be as simple as, 'Let us therefore give glory to God in the highest.' It should be noted that there is no penitential rite when baptism is celebrated within the Eucharist, since this would pre-empt the Decision. The Collect follows the Gloria, which may be that of the day or, if preferred, the form in CI, page 64, which is more appropriate at the principal service on Sunday than at a stand-alone celebration.

The Liturgy of the Word

Although the Liturgy of the Word can take exactly the same form as any other Sunday morning, if the celebration of baptism on a Sunday morning happens infrequently, it may be appropriate to take advantage of the freedom given by note 5 (CI: p. 99) and, at points in the year when this is permitted, give the whole liturgy a more distinctively baptismal flavour by going off piste and choosing readings appropriate to the occasion (for suggested passages, see CI: pp. 150–65, 167). Equally, if three readings and a psalm are the norm, depending on the length of the readings, it may be appropriate to reduce the number to two or even, in certain circumstances, to the

71

Gospel alone. As for the sermon, something short, informal and interactive may be most appropriate, particularly if there are enough children present to participate.

The Liturgy of Baptism

The Liturgy of Baptism is performed as described above (pp. 51–65). When making a decision about which texts are most appropriate, there is a stronger case for using the original CW forms than at a stand-alone celebration (unless the candidates include children who are able to answer for themselves), particularly if some of the baptismal party are themselves members of the Sunday congregation. To address the congregation as 'People of God' at the Presentation (CI: p. 66) does not sound out of place, and the question which it introduces is sufficiently direct to remind regular worshippers of their relationship with the candidate as fellow members of the body of Christ, as well as their responsibility towards him or her.

When it comes to the procession to the font (CI: p. 69), there will normally be a wider range of possibilities as to what music may accompany this than at a stand-alone celebration. Although organ music would suffice, it does not produce the same effect as the baptismal party being led through the congregation as they are singing. As an alternative to a hymn, song or, if there is a choir, a motet, to strengthen the sense of the candidate being baptized into a worshipping community which extends beyond earth to the church in heaven, and that he or she is supported by the prayers of both, the Thanksgiving for the Holy Ones of God (CI: pp. 174–6) or the litany of saints may be appropriate.

As for the order of the procession, in Eastertide a server or minister (the deacon, if there is one), carrying the Easter Candle, should lead the president and baptismal party. Depending on how much space is available, it may be best for other servers and clergy to remain where they are, except perhaps for the MC and/or someone to hold the book for the president. At other times in the year, the procession may be led by acolytes and a crucifer. The jug or ewer of water also needs to be brought to the font. If a godparent is going to pour the water into the font, they can also be asked to carry it. As the procession passes, all members of the congregation should be encouraged to face the font and, if possible, children should gather at the font so that they can see.

The celebration of baptism at the Eucharist may be an occasion when it is preferable to give the candle immediately after the anointing with chrism (CI: p. 71) rather than at the end of the rite (CI: p. 101, see note 17). This would be particularly appropriate if the candle(s) could be placed on the altar during the Eucharistic Prayer, and given back at the Dismissal. There are obviously practical considerations to bear in mind relating to the number of candidates and the size of the altar-table!

Whether or not the candle is given following baptism, CW suggests that the 'president and those who have been baptized may return from the font' at this point in the rite (CI: p. 71). The appropriateness of movement after baptism has already been discussed in relation to a stand-alone celebration. Obviously, at the Eucharist, staying at the font until the end of the service is not an option, but it may be best to wait until the Peace, so that the president and baptismal party can exchange the Peace with members of the congregation as they return to their places.

A decision also needs to be made about what form the Commission should take. Notwithstanding what has already been said about the original CW texts being preferred when the Sunday congregation is present, when it comes to the Commission, it would be preferable for the president to follow the ATAL guidelines and use his or her own words, appropriate to the style of the service, perhaps making a connection with what was said in the sermon. At a principal Sunday service, it is important not to forget that the Commission should be addressed to the congregation as well as the parents and godparents.

Since those planning the liturgy will need to be mindful of its overall length, there is something to be said for the Prayers of Intercession not taking the usual form, but being replaced by the president offering a short prayer for the candidates, parents and godparents at the end of the Commission, which can in turn lead into the Welcome and Peace. After the congregation has applauded the newly baptized, the president can introduce the Peace from the font, and the procession can return relatively informally while the offertory hymn starts. If some of the servers or other ministers have stayed behind, they can begin the preparation of the altar-table while this is happening. If the bread and wine for the Eucharist have been placed on a table near the font (once again, to highlight baptism and Eucharist as sacraments of initiation), these can be brought up in the procession from the font, possibly by communicant members of the baptismal party, if there are any, or other members of the congregation.

The Liturgy of the Eucharist and Sending Out

The Eucharist then continues as normal (with the baptismal candle(s) on the altar). In choosing which Eucharistic Prayer to use, the length and linguistic register of Prayer E may commend its use, even though the short Proper Preface (CI: p. 76) cannot be inserted into it. If Prayer G is chosen, prayer for the newly baptized may be offered within it. For example:

> Remember, Lord, *X* and *Y*
> who *have* been made *members* of your Church through baptism.
> Guide and protect *them* by the power of your Holy Spirit
> that *they* know your presence with *them*
> and witness to your love throughout *their lives*.

To shorten the communion rite, it may be appropriate to omit the *Agnus Dei*, or to sing it after the invitation. At the administration of communion, the baptismal party should be encouraged to come forward, if they would like to, whether or not they are going to receive communion. Turrell believes that 'it is very important that the newly baptized receive communion first' (Turrell 2013: p. 100). Pastorally, though, if the baptism party is willing to come forward, it is probably best to let others go first, so that the former have an example to follow. Once again, a 'Baptism Buddy' can help here. If communion is to be given to an infant, it may be administered in one or both kinds. If the child has been weaned, a tiny fragment of the host may be placed on the tongue (this is probably best done by a parent rather than the president). If the child has not been weaned, a small spoon or a (clean!) little finger may be used to communicate from the cup. To administer both elements together, a fragment of the host may be put onto the spoon with the wine, as is the custom in the Eastern Church. (For further guidance of communicating infants, see Turrell 2013: p. 134.)

Given what has already been fitted into the rite, it will be a kindness to children and parents if the service is concluded as expeditiously as possible. Trying to keep a period of silence after communion is likely to fail. Ablutions can be done after the service. One Prayer after Communion will suffice (CI: p. 76) and, if brief notices are to follow, these can include the Giving of a Lighted Candle, if this did not happen at the font; or, if it did, the candle may be returned to a parent or godparent, perhaps at the same time as they are given their cards and/or certificate. The service then concludes with the Blessing and Dismissal. If a hymn is normally sung before the Blessing, this may be an occasion to omit it or, exceptionally, for it to be sung as the procession leaves.

Infant baptism at a Service of the Word, Morning Prayer or Evening Prayer

If infants are baptized at a principal Sunday service, it is desirable for this to be a Eucharist (see pp. 66–70). Where this is not the case, CW provides notes on how baptism may be celebrated as part of a Service of the Word, Morning Prayer or Evening Prayer (CI: pp. 96–7). The basic principles of how the baptism rite may be celebrated, outlined in this chapter, can equally be applied in these situations.

Emergency Baptism

The rite of Emergency Baptism is published in three places (PS: pp. 195–8; CI: pp. 102–5; and, in its most easily accessible form, PMC: pp. 57–60). It goes without saying that great pastoral sensitivity needs to be exercised in the performance of this rite. The notes (CI: p. 105) explain that, if a person is in danger of death, a lay person may administer baptism, and that that person should subsequently inform the parish priest (note 1). They also make clear that, in the case of an infant, it is the responsibility of parents to request baptism (note 2), thereby implying that it should not be administered in response to a request from hospital staff or another relative or family friend. The same note goes on to say that parents 'should be assured that questions of ultimate salvation or of the provision of a Christian funeral for an infant who dies does not depend on whether or not the child has been baptized' (CI: p. 105). While an important theological point is being made here, the sort of emergency situation in which baptism is requested is rarely the time to embark upon such a discussion, and the minister should not question the parents' wishes if baptism is requested.

If an emergency baptism is administered in hospital, the advice of hospital staff should always be sought before beginning the service. If the minister is a priest or deacon, a white stole may be worn over the minister's clothes. If possible, the candidate's name should be ascertained before he or she is baptized, though if the name is unknown the baptism should not be delayed (CI: p. 105). In its simplest form, the rite requires water to be poured on the candidate while the Trinitarian formula is said (CI: p. 102). A minimal amount of water is likely to be most appropriate. Sterilized water may be provided by hospital staff, and it may be administered on a small piece of cotton wool. Whether any of the other liturgical elements provided are used will depend on individual circumstances. Oil should never be used with premature babies, as it can burn the skin.

If it appears likely that the newly baptized is nearing death, the minister may wish to wait with the family or return after a short period of time to use appropriate material from Ministry at the Time of Death (PS: pp. 216–35; PMC: pp. 63–87). (For resources for use when a child has died, see PMC: pp. 88–93.) If the newly baptized lives, when he or she is well enough to attend a service in church, the order for Holy Baptism is used, omitting the pre-baptismal signing, Prayer over the Water and the baptism itself (CI: p. 105, notes 4–7).

If, when parents request a baby to be baptized, and the child dies before the minister arrives, Nash suggests that it may be appropriate to offer a naming ceremony, in which oil rather than water is used, accompanied by the formula 'I name this child' (Nash 2011: pp. 144–5).

For further guidance on pastoral issues relating to the emergency baptism of babies, see Nash (2011), chapter 9. Additional liturgical resources can be found in Oliver (1996: p. 29), Nash (2011: pp. 162–4) and Ward (2012: pp. 38–40). When parish clergy administer baptism in hospital, they should always inform the chaplaincy team that they have done so.

5

The baptism and confirmation of adults

The principal focus of this chapter is the baptism and confirmation of adults within the context of the Eucharist. That said, it is important to recognize that such a service may include any combination of the following: the baptism of infants and children; the confirmation of those already baptized; the affirmation of baptismal faith of those already baptized and confirmed; and reception into the Church of England. Guidance on how to incorporate these will be given at the end of this chapter and in the next. In terms of setting and performance, a number of the points mentioned in relation to infants and children apply equally to adults and, where this is the case, will not be repeated here.

When preparing to host a celebration of adult initiation, a number of points need to be considered. With regard to anointing, two oils may be used in the combined rite of baptism and confirmation: the oil of baptism at the Signing with the Cross after the Decision, and the oil of chrism during the Confirmation (CI: p. 129, note 6). If the oil of baptism was used at the Call (see pp. 38–9), it is not used again during the baptism rite (CI: p. 37, note 3). As in other rites, to enable the congregation to see the oils, they should be kept in glass cruets or jugs and placed on tables near to where they will be used. (For further discussion on the use of oils in this rite, see CI: pp. 345–6, and ALG 4: pp. 45–9.)

If an adult is baptized by immersion, the candidate will need to bring a change of clothes to the service and these should be left in a suitable place for the candidate to change after baptism (perhaps in a nearby room or behind a screen) together with a towel and an alb, if one is to be worn as the baptismal garment (see p. 89). If the president or another minister enters the water to baptize, another changing room/screen will be required (see p. 13).

When thinking about the use of the space, if the building has a font, it should be used, if at all possible (see pp. 3–6), unless a pool is installed for baptism by immersion. In this rite, consideration also needs to be given to where confirmation is administered. After baptism, CW directs that 'the bishop and candidates gather at the place of confirmation' (CI: p. 118), without giving guidance on where this might be, except that 'the places where baptism and confirmation are administered should be determined after consultation between the bishop and the parish priest' (CI: p. 128). Most commonly, if baptism is administered at the font, the procession returns to the chancel step or sanctuary for confirmation. If this happens, it is important not to give the impression that baptism is, in any way, a preliminary to confirmation. On more than one occasion, as they are about to confirm, bishops have been heard to say, 'And now we come to the moment when the candidates receive the gift of the Spirit'! To celebrate confirmation at the place where baptism has been administered allows the former to be presented as a post-baptismal hand-laying and anointing, rather than a separate rite with a theology which conflicts with that of baptism. If this is possible, it underlines the important theological principle that, whatever view is taken about the meaning of confirmation, it is always derived from, and does not add to, baptism (see CI: p. 348).

In many traditions it has been customary for the bishop to sit to confirm. As previously mentioned, the chair from which the bishop presides should be the chair normally used by the president (see p. 8). If the bishop presides over the Liturgy of Initiation from that chair, there are points at which it may be appropriate to sit (see pp. 11–12). However, when not at the font, it is often appropriate for the bishop to stand in a central position, perhaps at the chancel step, facing the congregation, in a space in which there is room for the candidates and sponsors to stand between the bishop and the congregation.

Since this is an episcopal rite, it is important to consult the bishop when planning the service, and to make sure the bishop's office has a draft of the service booklet in good time so that comments and subsequent changes can be made. Many diocesan websites publish their bishop's preferred version of the initiation services. These provide a useful starting point, but the parish priest also has a responsibility to discuss with the bishop how it can be adapted to fit both the liturgical space and the tradition of the parish. A one-size-fits-all model is rarely optimal, and runs the risk of resulting in a liturgy that is bland and uninspiring. If possible, the booklet should contain all the texts that the congregation will need, including the hymns and songs, and omit the presidential texts, which can be included in a folder prepared for the bishop. The booklet should also include the names of the candidates and their sponsors and, if space permits, a short account, in the candidates' own words, of their journey to baptism (CI: p. 129, note 3). This is particularly appropriate if testimony is not given within the rite. Since this is an occasion when there are likely to be a number of people present who are not regular churchgoers, it may also be an opportunity to advertise the parish's services and activities, as well as any future discipleship courses. Parishes may also want to produce prayer cards for people to take home with them.

A rehearsal before the initiation of adults is essential, and will normally help to reduce levels of anxiety (among candidates and clergy!) on the day, leaving the parish priest free to walk through the service with the bishop. It is important, however, that the candidates have an opportunity to meet the bishop before the service. Some bishops like to see candidates individually; others may want to meet them as a group. To help the candidates remember the different points during the service at which they have to move or turn, a specially annotated order of service can be given to them at the rehearsal or they can add their own notes to a congregational copy.

On the day, sponsors should be on hand to welcome their candidate and his or her guests and show them to their seats. Where the candidates sit will depend on how many of them there are as well as the layout of the building. In some cases it may be appropriate for them to sit together at the front of the church with their sponsors next to them or in the row behind. Alternatively, each candidate may sit with their family, friends and sponsor, preferably at the end of a row so that it is easy for them to come forward at the appropriate time.

A final practical consideration relates to the eucharistic elements, and ensuring that there is sufficient bread and wine for communion. At services such as this it is often difficult to predict what proportion of the congregation will communicate. In addition to the bread and wine that is brought up in the offertory procession, further supplies should be placed on the credence table, so that they can be used, if necessary. After the Peace, the parish priest or another minister will need to make a decision about how much should be consecrated. If any of the consecrated elements are not required for communion, they can be consumed after the service or reserved. If the elements prove insufficient, CW directs that more should be consecrated (CWMV: p. 296), although if there are sufficient hosts reserved from a previous celebration to complete communion, it would seem expedient to use these. (On the theological and liturgical issues related to this, see ALG 3: pp. 58, 75.)

Structure and content

The basic template for this service is Baptism and Confirmation within a Celebration of Holy Communion (CI: pp.108–23). As with infants, it is important to have a sense of the overall structure, how the various elements relate to each other, where alternative positions are permitted, and which parts are optional. Mirroring other CW rites, initiation is celebrated within a eucharistically shaped service in response to the proclamation of God's word:

Table 5.1 Order for the baptism and confirmation of adults

	Mandatory	*Optional*
℣ Preparation		
		Entrance Hymn
	The Greeting	
		Introduction
		Gloria in excelsis
	The Collect	
℣ The Liturgy of the Word		
		Reading(s)
		Gospel Acclamation
	Gospel reading	
	Sermon	
℣ The Liturgy of Initiation		
	Presentation of the Candidates	
	The Decision	
	The Signing with the Cross	

Table 5.1 (*cont'd*)

	Mandatory	Optional
		Procession to the Font
	Prayer over the Water	
	Profession of Faith	
	Baptism	
		Procession to the place of Confirmation
	Confirmation	
		Commission
		Prayers of Intercession
	Welcome and Peace	
¶ The Liturgy of the Eucharist		
		Offertory Hymn
	Preparation of the Table	
	Taking of the Bread and Wine	
	The Eucharistic Prayer	
	The Lord's Prayer	
	Breaking of the Bread	
	Giving of Communion	
	Prayer after Communion	
¶ The Sending Out		
		Final hymn
		The Blessing
		Giving of a Candle
	The Dismissal	

As with the rite when used for infants, the Presentation of the Candidates is optional but the questions that follow it are not (CI: p. 111). Unlike the infant rite, the notes do not permit the Presentation to take place between the Greeting and the Collect, but they do allow for the candidate to be signed with the cross after baptism rather than following the Decision (CI: p. 129, note 7). However, given the proximity of the later position to confirmation, the avoidance of confusion between the two rites could be considered sufficiently strong grounds for not signing after baptism. In any case, when a candidate is signed following the Decision (the default position), chrism is not used to accompany the post-baptismal prayer (CI: p. 129, note 6). At the Profession of Faith, there is no alternative to the interrogative form of the Apostles' Creed. Curiously, whereas when infants are baptized the Commission must be included after Baptism, at the beginning of the Sending Out, or within the sermon, for adults this is not the case, implying that it carries less weight. It may be used after confirmation or at the beginning of the Sending Out or be omitted altogether. It is not clear whether making it optional was deliberate or is an error. What does appear to be a mistake is the structure page not indicating that the Blessing is optional (CI: p. 107), since this is indicated by the relevant rubric (CI: p. 122). The Giving of a Lighted Candle is optional and may take place after baptism instead of before the Dismissal.

A final point needs to be made about the use of ATAL. Although these texts were devised in response to a request to provide appropriate resources for the baptism of infants (see p. xix), legally there is no impediment to them being used for the combined rite of baptism and confirmation if it is deemed appropriate in the local context. This is something to discuss with the bishop when the service is being planned.

Preparation

The liturgy begins with the entrance procession. It is helpful if at least some of the hymns are familiar to visitors, and a strong start to the service is important. If the Eucharist is concelebrated, the concelebrating priests walk in pairs in front of the bishop. If there is a deacon of the rite, he or she walks in front of the concelebrants, carrying the Gospel Book. If not, it may be carried by one of the concelebrants or another minister. If the procession includes clergy who are not concelebrants, they follow the servers or choir, preceded by any lay ministers. It is normally helpful if a minister, lay or ordained, acts as the bishop's chaplain. This person walks behind the bishop (wearing a cotta or surplice and, if a priest, a stole). (For further guidance on the bishop as president, see pp. 11–12, and ALG 3: pp. 14–15, 21.)

The Preparation begins with a dialogue between the bishop and the people before the Greeting (CI: p. 108). Since 'other suitable words' are also permitted, a simplified form may be preferred:

> In the name of the Father,
> and of the Son,
> and of the Holy Spirit.

All **Amen.**

> Peace be with you

All **and also with you.**

During Eastertide, the Easter Acclamation may follow.

Using his or her own words, the bishop then introduces the service and, on a day on which the *Gloria in excelsis* is appointed, it may be sung, introduced by 'Let us therefore give glory to God in the highest', or a previously agreed form of words, which give a clear signal for it to begin. The Collect follows and, as the rubric suggests, on Sundays, Principal Feasts, other Principal Holy Days and Festivals, it should normally be the Collect of the Day. On other occasions, the text provided or one of the seasonal alternatives may be preferred (CI: p. 109 and p. 129, note 5).

Liturgy of the Word

When infants are baptized at the Eucharist, there may be good reason to reduce the number of readings, perhaps even to the Gospel alone. When all the candidates are adults, although care needs to be taken not to create a rite that is unreasonably long, a substantial engagement with Scripture is appropriate. The Liturgy of the Word may therefore follow the normal Sunday pattern or, if there are usually three readings and a psalm, one reading before the Gospel may suffice. Guidance given as to whether the readings should be those of the day or others chosen for the occasion mirrors that for the Collect (CI: p. 110). If a Gospel Acclamation normally precedes the Gospel reading, this may be sung, or a hymn, particularly one which has Alleluia in the refrain, may be preferred, and the final verse may be sung after the Gospel has been proclaimed. When choosing who to read, if a number of churches have come together for the service, it is important to involve people from each congregation during the course of the rite (as readers, ministers of communion, etc.). If a deacon is present, he or she should read the Gospel.

The bishop is principal minister of word as well as sacrament. This point can be expressed in two ways: first, after the Gospel, the book may be brought to the bishop to kiss, after which the bishop may turn to the people and bless them with it (see ALG 3: p. 46); second, although the bishop is at liberty to ask another authorized minister to preach, the sermon is an important opportunity for the bishop's teaching ministry to be exercised (the bishop is also chief catechist), and for the relationship between the bishop and the local community to be strengthened through it. Wherever possible, the bishop should preach from a place where sight lines are good and the candidates are clearly visible.

The Liturgy of Initiation

Presentation of the Candidates

The Liturgy of Initiation begins with the Presentation of the Candidates (CI: p. 111). After the sermon, the bishop stands in a central position (or at the chair, see p. 78) with the book-bearer and chaplain. If there is room, they may be joined by any local and visiting clergy who have been involved in the candidates' catechesis, but not so that the space becomes overcrowded: the focus needs to be on the candidates and the bishop. The bishop faces the people, with the candidates and their sponsors facing the bishop. Whether the congregation stands or sits for the Presentation will depend on the number of candidates, and if any of them are going to give testimony. If the congregation remains seated, they should stand when the bishop addresses them at the end of the Presentation. For guidance on when the mitre should be worn and the crozier carried, see pages 11–12. If a server or other minister holds the book for the bishop, the chaplain can hold the mitre and crozier when they are not being worn. Alternatively, one or two servers may do this, leaving the chaplain free to hold the book.

Each candidate may be presented by their sponsor. Although this is optional, there is much to commend it, not least since it gives liturgical visibility to candidates and sponsors early on in the rite. If a microphone is used, the sponsors may stand at the lectern / legilium, or another convenient place, to present their candidate before moving to join him or her. As the candidates are presented, they may turn, one by one, to face the people. As with the catechumenal rites, the presentation is made to the whole congregation, not just to the president. The following, or other similar words, may be used:

> Brothers and sisters, *N* has been exploring the Way of Christ
> with us.
> I now present *him* to be baptized and confirmed.

Once all the candidates have been presented, they turn to face the bishop to be asked if they wish to be baptized, and whether they are ready to affirm their faith in Christ. The candidates answer together, after which individual testimony by the candidates may follow (CI: p. 129, note 3). While such a public display of faith may be frowned upon by some traditions, when done well, testimony can be a power-ful witness to the activity of God in the candidates' lives. There may be pastoral sensitivities around which of the candidates wishes to speak (some may feel more comfortable than others; none should feel coerced or excluded). If there is a large number, and timing is likely to be an issue, those giving testimony can be asked to prepare, together with their sponsor, a short paragraph explaining why they feel called to baptism, and they can read this out. Once again, to use a microphone, candidates may move to the lectern/legilium or another place where they are visible to the congregation, or a hand-held microphone can be passed between them.

The candidates then turn to face the congregation again as the bishop addresses the people, now standing, asking them to express their welcome and support for the candidates. When the baptism rite is used for adults, the theology of prevenient grace is less strongly expressed than it is for infants (see p. 52). Up until this point, the emphasis has been on the candidates and what they desire. This final question redresses the balance somewhat (if this has not already happened in any testimony that is given), emphasizing faith as God's gift, and baptism as the means by which God calls people into the household of faith. The same emphasis is found in ATAL, which may be preferred. After the congregation has responded, the candidates turn to face the bishop for the Decision.

The Decision

The congregation remains standing for the Decision (CI: p. 112) and sponsors may wish to place a hand on the shoulder of their candidate in support for them as they answer the bishop's questions. Turrell makes a helpful point about eye contact during this part of the rite. ALG 3 suggests that both the use of the voice and the eyes will be affected by whether the president is addressing God or the congregation (ALG 3: p. 6). In this connection, Turrell notes:

> The questions asked of the candidates in baptism are life-changing. The celebrant needs to treat them as real questions asked of real people

who might really say no, rather than rote recitation. That means looking at the person to whom one is speaking.

(Turrell 2013: p. 90)

Having someone hold the book will help the bishop engage directly with the candidates. As for which text to use, since the order of questions in the form on page 168 of CI is problematic (see p. 53), the choice is between the original CW version and ATAL. For most adults, the richer language of the former will make it the preferred version, particularly if it has been studied as part of the candidates' preparation. Given that the candidates may have already turned 180 degrees on a couple of occasions, to turn again in the middle of the Decision, as suggested by ATAL, seems unnecessary and potentially confusing, since the point of it would not be to face the congregation, as it has been previously. Furthermore, at this point in the rite, it is probably best for the bishop to remain in a central position throughout. As for the 'large candle' which may be lit at the Decision, the suggestion is that, as with infants, the Easter Candle should be lit before the service starts, and stand next to the font or, during Eastertide, beside the altar (see p. 43). A proliferation of symbolic actions runs the risk of detracting from the power of what is being said here. The remainder of the rite is not lacking in symbolism!

Signing with the Cross

The first of these symbolic actions is the Signing with the Cross (CI: p. 113). A server or other minister approaches during the Decision and, when it has finished, may pour some of the oil of baptism from a glass jug or cruet into the bishop's cupped hand or a shallow dish, from where it can be taken to anoint the candidates. If there are a large number of candidates, a dish is likely to be a more practical option. At this point, the bishop may approach the candidates or they can come, one by one, to the bishop, accompanied by their sponsor. To personalize this moment, the bishop may insert the person's name at the beginning of the formula. If it can be agreed in advance in what order the candidates will stand or approach, the names can appear in this order in the bishop's folder. If that's not possible, the parish priest, standing to one side of the bishop, can say each name to the bishop sotto voce before the candidate is anointed. After the bishop has made the sign of the cross in oil on the candidate's forehead, the parish priest and the sponsor may do the same (without saying anything). Once all the candidates have been anointed, a lavabo will be needed for the bishop's hands to be cleansed before the bishop addresses the candidates and the people respond, using the form in the main CW text or ATAL. In the prayer that follows, the bishop's hands may be extended, palms down, towards the candidates.

A procession forms and moves to the font. For guidance on what may accompany this, see page 72. A further alternative is the litany from the American rite (BCP 1979: pp. 305–6), which may be read or chanted in procession by a deacon or another minister (lay or ordained), either on its own or after the litany of the saints. In Eastertide a server or minister (the deacon, if not leading the litany), carrying the Easter Candle, should lead the procession, followed by a server carrying a jug or ewer of water, the book-bearer, clergy (if there is room for them to gather around the font), the bishop, chaplain and, finally, the candidates accompanied by their sponsors. Outside the Easter season, the procession may be led by acolytes and crucifer. As the procession passes, all members of the congregation turn to face the font. If there is enough space for any children present to gather round the font, this is desirable, although it's important that clergy, servers, children and candidates are so arranged that the candidates are able to stand next to the font, and the view of the rest of the congregation is not obstructed. If baptism is to be administered by immersion, this is a good moment for candidates to remove their footwear (and anything else that they want to take off before they are baptized) and, if the minister of baptism is going to enter the water with the candidates, for footwear and vestments to be removed, leaving the alb and pectoral cross.

Prayer over the Water

Once all have gathered, water is poured into the font or baptismal pool (in which there should already be a substantial amount of water) so that it is full to the brim or, even, overflowing. This could be done by the server who carried it in the procession. Alternatively, a sponsor or, if there are candidates from a number of parishes, a visiting parish priest could be invited to assist. Whoever pours the water, the action must be able to be seen and heard. Turrell mentions the importance of silence being kept during this 'so that the sound of the rushing water may fill the room' (Turrell 2013: p. 91).

The bishop then stands at the font to say or sing the Prayer over the Water (the Roman Rite and BCP 1979 provide chants to which one of the CW texts may be set), the book being held by the chaplain or a server. Here there would seem to be little justification for using ATAL. The bishop uses the manual acts as described on page 58.

Profession of Faith

The bishop addresses the whole congregation and asks them, together with the candidates, to make the Profession of Faith. If, during their preparation for baptism, the Apostles' Creed was presented to the candidates (*traditio symboli*) for study and discussion, they now have the opportunity to read it back (*redditio symboli*) (see pp. 40–1). To articulate this link between the catechumenate and the rite of baptism within the process of Christian initiation, a slight alteration may be made to the bishop's words of introduction. Addressing the candidates, the bishop may say:

> My brothers and sisters, in preparation for your baptism
> the Christian community presented you with the Apostles' Creed,
> the profession of faith.
> I now invite you to join them in professing together
> the faith of the Church.

The Apostles' Creed follows (CI: p. 115).

Baptism

CW allows the bishop to delegate the administration of baptism to another minister (see pp. 9–10). Where this happens, it is important that the sense of the bishop's presidency over the rite is maintained. If candidates from a number of parishes are to be baptized at the service, it may be appropriate for each to be baptized by their own parish priest.

After the Profession of Faith, the bishop, standing at the font, turns to the first candidate and, addressing them by name, asks if this is their faith (CI: p. 116). Again, eye contact is important. Even if another minister baptizes, the bishop should ask this question. The candidate replies, and then moves to the font. He or she may be followed by his or her sponsor, but the sponsor does not lead the candidate to the font; the candidate needs to be seen to be making this part of the journey of his or her own free will in response to the call and grace of God. The candidate leans over the font, and the bishop (or other minister) pours water on the candidate, saying the formula clearly and slowly, to which all respond 'Amen'. In order to use a substantial amount of water (CI: p. 100, note 12; strangely, reference to this is not included in the notes for the combined rite of Baptism and Confirmation), the water may be poured over the candidate's head from the same jug or ewer that was used earlier in the rite. A shell or cupped hand will not produce the same effect.

If baptism is by immersion, the minister of baptism enters the pool at the end of the Profession of Faith. After the candidate has answered the bishop's question, he or she joins the minister, assisted, if necessary, by the sponsor. The minister supports the candidate's back while immersing him or her three times in the water and, simultaneously, saying the formula. Alternatively, Turner suggests that the candidate kneels in the water and is then brought face down into the water three times as the persons of the Trinity are named (Turner 2007: p. 109). Whichever method is use, the recitation of the formula should be done from memory so that a book is not required!

When baptism is by affusion, the newly baptized should be given a towel as they walk away from the font. If there is more than one candidate, the bishop puts the question to the next in line, and the sequence is repeated. Any temptation to hurry needs to be resisted so that sufficient time can be given to each candidate. When baptism is administered by immersion, the sponsor may help the candidate out of the pool and give him or her a towel as he or she moves to the changing area.

CW permits the newly baptized to be 'clothed with a white robe' (CI: p.116; p. 130, note 10). If they have been baptized by immersion, a change of clothes will be necessary anyway; if not, a robe can be put on over the clothes they are already wearing. An alb is an obvious choice for a white robe, evoking 'the imagery of the saints robed in white, washed in the blood of the Lamb, in Revelation 7' (Turrell 2013: p. 95). If this is to happen, a hymn, song or chant may be sung while the sponsors help the candidates to put on the albs. This may also be an appropriate time for the bishop to sprinkle the whole congregation with baptismal water (unless the bishop has administered baptism by immersion and needs to change, in which case another minister may do this). Although CW suggests that only candidates for confirmation, affirmation and/or reception may sign themselves with water or be sprinkled, the sprinkling of the whole assembly is a powerful way of associating them with what has just happened and reminding them of their own baptism. There is no need to use a formula during the sprinkling but, if one is required, 'Remember your baptism into Christ Jesus' would be appropriate. An aspergilium, brush or, preferably, a large sprig of rosemary dipped into a bowl or bucket from which water has been drawn from the font may be used, so that the sprinkling can be smelled as well as felt. After the sprinkling, the newly baptized, wearing their white robes, stand before the bishop, who says to them 'You have been clothed with Christ . . .' (CI: p. 116) before inviting the whole congregation to pray and, after a short period of silence, saying the concluding prayer (CI: p. 117) with hands in the *orans* position. If the candidates are not clothed in a white robe, and no change of clothes is required, the sprinkling follows the baptism.

Nothing, as yet, has been said about the pneumatic post-baptismal prayer which follows the optional clothing (CI: p. 116). Given that confirmation is to follow immediately, it seems unnecessary and, indeed, confusing for the bishop to pray for God to renew the newly baptized 'by his anointing spirit' minutes before the same Spirit is invoked to 'rest upon them'. It is therefore suggested that it is omitted. If it is used, it must not be accompanied by anointing with chrism (CI: p. 129, note 6).

Confirmation

What happens next will depend on where confirmation is going to be administered (see p. 78). If it is to happen in the same place as the Presentation, Decision and Signing, a procession is formed in the same order as before. During the procession, a hymn, chant or song may be sung. Chants such as *Veni sancte spiritus* or *Veni creator* should be avoided in case they are thought to imply that the Holy Spirit is only now going to make an appearance! If Confirmation happens at the font, depending on the layout of the building, the bishop and candidates may need to regroup. Ideally, there needs to be enough space for the bishop to face the candidates and the congregation, the latter standing in arc or semi-circle. At this point, sponsors may step aside or, if the procession has returned to the front of the church, walk with the newly baptized and then return to their places.

It is customary for candidates to kneel to be confirmed, but the rite does not require this; nor does it suggest that the congregation should kneel. If there is sufficient space, the bishop and candidates may remain standing throughout and, depending on how many candidates there are, it may be preferable for the congregation to stand as well (if there is a large number, the congregation should kneel or sit, the order of service encouraging them to pray for the candidates). Any decision on posture will need to be made bearing in mind the relative heights of the bishop and candidates, since the bishop needs to be able to reach each candidate's head to anoint and lay on hands. A choice also has to be made about whether the bishop goes to the candidates to confirm or the candidates approach the bishop. Here it is suggested that it is the bishop who moves, approaching each candidate one at a time. If the candidates are to kneel, it may be possible for hassocks to be put in place during the baptism so that they are already in position when the procession returns. If confirmation is administered at the font, the same could happen during the sprinkling.

The Confirmation begins with the ancient prayer drawing on Isaiah 11.2–3a. The bishop's hands remained joined for the responses that introduce it. They are then extended, palms down, towards the candidates for the prayer itself, and brought together again during the last line before the people respond with the 'Amen'. The bishop's folder will need to be held by the chaplain or a server to make these gestures possible. As has already been mentioned, there is sometimes a temptation for the bishop to use his or her own words to introduce the Confirmation and, thereby, inadvertently suggest that this hand-laying and anointing are of greater significance than baptism. Since the intention here is to present confirmation as a post-baptismal rite, it is probably best to let the texts and accompanying ritual action speak for themselves without any additional commentary.

Note 6 (CI: p. 129) is unambiguous in permitting the oil of chrism to be used to accompany confirmation. Less clear, however, is its guidance on when and how it may be administered. Given the spectrum of belief regarding the rite, this may be deliberate! Experience suggests that bishops fall into two camps: some anoint as they address the candidate, 'God has called you by name and made you his own'. However if, as the commentary suggests, anointing is an accompaniment to prayer (CI: p. 345), it seems strange for chrism to be administered during a descriptive rather than performative or petitionary statement. Others follow the Roman Rite and, after the laying on of hands, anoint with chrism while addressing the candidate with the performative formula, 'Be sealed with the gift of the Spirit.' Here the genre of the liturgical formula used to accompany the anointing is more appropriate, but it expresses a stronger relationship between the anointing and the pneumatic gift than many Anglicans would find acceptable, and does not reflect the overall theology of the rite. In an imperfect liturgical world, the first option may be the best solution, not least since it can be seen to affirm the identity of the newly baptized as one who has been born again by water and the Spirit and now seeks prayer for the ongoing activity of God's anointing and strengthening Spirit in his or her life. (For further discussion on this, see ALG 4: p. 48.)

In terms of performance, Turrell suggests two methods of post-baptismal chrismation: in one the chrism is poured directly onto the head of the newly baptized and used to sign the forehead; in the other, chrism is poured into one of the president's hands who, from there, smears it on the head and forehead of the candidate, before signing the forehead with the cross (Turrell 2013: p. 96). The main point to notice with these suggestions is that they envisage a much more generous use of oil than is currently commonly practised, and also place as much emphasis on anointing the crown of the head as on making the sign of the cross:

> When the chrism is used, it should be used in abundance, so that all may see (and smell) it. Baptism and its associated rites should overwhelm the senses – of touch, of hearing, of smell, and (at communion) of taste. The more oil used in chrismation, the better.
>
> (Turrell 2013: p. 97)

Such extravagance may be too much for some, but it is worth thinking again about how this anointing is administered, and how it can be performed so that it differs ritually from the pre-baptismal signing. Repeating the same action again (the Roman practice of a simple sign of the cross on the forehead) is less than ideal. One variation on Turrell's suggestions would be to pour the oil onto the candidate's head: not so much that it runs down the face and drips onto clothes; but enough so that it can be seen and smelled as it is being poured, then smeared onto the head and, if desired, used to make the sign of the cross, either on the crown of the head or on the forehead, before the hand-laying.

In connection with the hand-laying, although CW refers to the bishop's hand in the singular, it is common for both hands to be used at this point. A server with the vessel of oil will need to precede or follow the bishop as he or she moves from candidate to candidate. The server should also carry a towel for the bishop to use and to deal with any drips, and another server should be waiting with a lavabo. If the bishop has memorized the two formulas, there is no need for anyone to hold the book, unless a text is needed for the candidates' names. Alternatively, the parish priest can speak the names sotto voce, as at the signing.

The confirmation takes place in silence, and concludes with the classic Anglican confirmation prayer, which, in CW, is used as a congregational text (the candidates should be reminded at the rehearsal that this a prayer said for them, not by them). Here the bishop may want to introduce it in his or her own words, encouraging the people to use it to gather together their prayers for the candidates. At the end of the prayer, if they have been kneeling or sitting, the candidates and congregation are invited to stand.

Commission, Prayers, Welcome and Peace

The Commission (CI: p. 119), based on the second part of the American baptismal covenant (BCP 1979: pp. 304–5), is optional. If it is used, it may follow the confirmation or be inserted at the beginning of the Sending Out. It is entirely appropriate for the candidates to be asked to respond to their initiation into Christ and his Church in this way, and its use should be encouraged. However, since the Eucharist is also a sacrament of initiation, to place the Commission at the end of the rite may be more desirable. If the Prayers of Intercession are omitted (which, in a potentially long rite that consists of many prayers, is nearly always the best option), the Confirmation leads straight into the Welcome and Peace.

At the Welcome, the candidates may face the bishop as they are addressed, and then turn to the congregation as the latter respond, 'We welcome you . . .' (CI: p. 120). Applause follows, after which the candidates turn back to the bishop as the Peace is introduced. The deacon, if there is one, invites people to exchange a sign of peace. The bishop should be sure to greet all the newly baptized; sponsors, parish clergy, friends and family should be given time to do the same.

The Liturgy of the Eucharist

If the candidates are able to make their way to the back of the church while sharing the peace, they may process back together, the front pair carrying the bread and wine for the Eucharist, before returning to their places. If Eucharistic Prayer A, B or C is chosen, the short Proper Preface (CI: p. 121) may be used. In Prayer G, prayer for the newly baptized may be included. The following suggestion draws on the language of the post-baptismal prayer on page 116, and would be suitable here if, as has been suggested, it is omitted earlier in the rite:

> Remember, Lord, *N* and *N*
> who *have* been made *members* of your Church through baptism.
> Within the company of Christ's pilgrim people
> may *they* daily be renewed by his anointing Spirit
> until *they* come to the inheritance of your saints in glory.

At the baptism of adults, it is appropriate to invite the candidates to receive first. If this service attracts a much larger number of communicants than normal, it may be advisable for communion to be administered in more than one place, and for the ablutions to be left until after the service.

If possible, a short period of silence may be kept at the end of communion (after any music has finished) before the bishop stands to say the Prayer after Communion. Even if the Collect of the Day was used in the Preparation, the prayer on page 121 may be considered an appropriate Post Communion throughout the year.

The Sending Out
Commission

If, as suggested, the Commission takes place here, the candidates stand facing the bishop (attended by the book-bearer and chaplain), as they did at the Presentation, and respond to the questions that are put to them. Indeed, it may be preferable for the Post Communion to be led from here as well, so that the bishop does not have to change position between the two. Whenever the bishop moves, if he or she is not going to return to the altar at the end of the rite, the altar may first be kissed. To emphasize the Eucharist as a sacrament of initiation, a small insertion may be made in the first line:

> Those who are baptized and fed at the Lord's table
> are called to worship and serve God.

This leads nicely into the first of the questions, which talks of continuing 'in the breaking of bread, and in the prayers' (CI: p. 119). Since the Blessing follows the Commission, the commentary suggests amending the final prayer so that it can lead straight into the Blessing (CI: p. 338). Although possible, the problem with making this change is that the Commission, including the final prayer, relates to the newly baptized, whereas the Blessing is of the whole congregation. Furthermore, to place the Blessing between the Commission and the Giving of the Lighted Candle often feels awkward, probably because a blessing normally indicates the conclusion of a service. The suggestion here is to reorder the Sending Out as follows:

- Commission
- Giving of a Lighted Candle
- Blessing
- Dismissal.

Giving of a Lighted Candle

CW encourages candles to be given during the Sending Out, but this may also happen immediately following baptism or after the candidates have been clothed (CI: p. 131, note 14). The main advantage of the earlier position is that it creates a strong association between baptism and illumination (it is, after all, not by being given a candle that the candidates receive the light of Christ, but through the grace of baptism). If given at the end of the rite, the candle symbolizes 'the apostolic summons to shine in the world, which is appropriate to the Sending Out of the whole people of God' (CI: p. 338).

If the candles are given after baptism, it is often problematic to keep them alight until the end of the rite unless, as previously suggested, all the baptismal candles can be put on the altar during the Liturgy of the Eucharist, or in a pricket stand or tray of sand, perhaps in front of an icon or statue, and then given back to the candidates, possibly during the final hymn (see p. 73).

If the candle is given during the Sending Out, outside Eastertide the Easter Candle will need to be carried from the font. This may be done in a hymn following the Post Communion Prayer, and carried by a deacon or another minister. During Eastertide, if the stand for the Easter Candle is in the sanctuary, and the Sending Out happens elsewhere, it can again be brought to where it is needed. Other ministers or servers assist the bishop by lighting the baptismal candles from the Easter Candle. Or, if preferred, the candidates' own parish priest or their sponsor may give the candle before the bishop addresses the candidates together (CI: p. 122) and gives the blessing. Mirroring the prayer of confirmation, the responses in note 13 (CI: p. 130) may introduce the blessing, and these may be prefaced with the greeting 'The Lord be with you' and its response.

The Dismissal, said with hands joined by the deacon or, if not, the bishop, concludes the rite, and the procession then leaves in the usual way, the bishop leading the newly baptized through the congregation. Applause may be appropriate as the procession passes through the congregation, particularly if it did not happen at the Welcome.

The baptism of infants and adults

The baptism of infants and adults within the same liturgy is particularly fitting where members of the same family are baptized, but may also be appropriate on other occasions, particularly when parents who are regular churchgoers wish to have a child baptized.

The starting point is the rite of Baptism and Confirmation within Holy Communion (CI: pp. 108–23) to which several adaptations are made (CI: p. 128, see note 1.). When putting together this service, the primary consideration needs to be that infant baptism is, in no way, presented as inferior to adult baptism (CI: p. 333). Furthermore, whereas the presence of infants does not require a dumbing-down of the rite, concern for the overall length of the service may justify omitting any spoken testimony (it can be provided in written form in the service booklet) and reducing the number of readings.

Infants, with their parents and godparents, should sit with the other candidates. They are brought forward at the Presentation and may be presented by a godparent. After the bishop has asked the congregation if they will support and uphold the candidates (CI: p. 111), the questions to parents and godparents (CI: p. 66) follow. When it comes to the Decision, parents and godparents answer for the children. If parents are to be baptized at the same time as their children, they answer in the first person plural: 'We reject . . .' or 'We do', if using ATAL (CI: p. 128, note 1). Infants are signed at the same time as adults. If the adult candidates include either or both parents, they should be signed first, and then sign their children with the godparents, if they wish.

At the baptism itself, children may be baptized immediately after their parents, if they are also candidates, or before or after the adult candidates. If the post-baptismal prayer (CI: p. 116) is not used for adults (see p. 90) it is always used for infants, during which the bishop may pour chrism over the head of the child (see pp. 61–2) while he or she is being held over the water. To make it clear that this is the same oil that will be used in the confirmation of adults, it should be carried to the place of confirmation, if confirmation is not going to happen near the font, rather than using two different vessels for the chrism. At Holy Communion, if the infant is not going to receive (see pp. 69–70), he or she should be brought forward to receive a blessing when the adult candidates make their first communion. The baptism candle is presented at the same time as candles are given to the other candidates (either after baptism or during the Sending Out). At the Commission, rather than trying to combine two separate forms, the bishop may wish to address parents and godparents at the same time as the adult candidates by using his or her own words. This would give a strong signal that 'there is only one baptism which brings people into relationship with Christ and his Church' (CI: p. 333), and that it carries with it the same lifelong responsibilities.

Adult baptism (without confirmation) at the Sunday Eucharist

If there is a very strong pastoral reason (besides baptism *in extremis*, for which the rite of Emergency Baptism is provided; CI: pp. 102–5) for not celebrating adult initiation as a combined episcopal rite of baptism and confirmation within the context of the Eucharist, the baptism of adults may be administered by a priest or deacon. Wherever possible, such a baptism should take place at a principal service at which the newly baptized make their first communion. The rite is that for Holy Baptism (CI: pp. 63–77) supplemented by the additional guidance given in CI: pp. 78–9).

The Preparation, Liturgy of the Word and Liturgy of Baptism are celebrated as described above. If the candidates include infants as well as adults, the relevant adaptations to the rite are made. The post-baptismal prayer and its associated anointing with chrism should be used for all candidates. It is probably best for this to happen as each candidate is standing at the font, or in the baptism pool, the minister of baptism pouring the oil over the crown of his or her head so that it drips into the water. Pertinent, in this connection, is the commentary's statement that 'chrism may be used more than once in a person's journey of faith' (CI: p. 343), but not more than once for the same person in a service. The baptism candle is given at this service, either immediately after baptism or during the Sending Out. If confirmation is to follow within a relatively short period of time, it is probably best not to use the form of the Commission which will most likely be used on that occasion. Instead, it would be better for the president to use his or her own words. The Welcome and Peace may happen at the font (the Prayers of Intercession having been omitted) and then the newly baptized can exchange the peace with the congregation as they walk back to their places. Alternatively, having greeted people, they may return to the font, and bring forward the bread and wine during the offertory hymn. If Eucharistic Prayer G is used, the intercession suggested above (see p. 94) is appropriate. At the end of the rite, the president may lead the candidates through the church after the Dismissal.

Baptism and confirmation with confirmation of those already baptized

A service of adult initiation will often include, alongside candidates for baptism and confirmation, candidates for confirmation (only) who have previously been baptized. These can easily be incorporated into the rite, as long as they are not confused with the candidates for baptism. Some of the confirmation candidates may already be communicants; others may not be. When discussing the service with the bishop's office, it is important that the bishop is made aware of these details to avoid any confusion on the day.

The rite is that for Baptism and Confirmation within Holy Communion (CI: pp. 108–23). CW orders the Presentation as follows (CI: p. 111):

- Presentation of all candidates
- Question to candidates for baptism
- Question to candidates for confirmation (only)
- Optional testimony by all candidates
- Question to whole congregation.

In order to distinguish more clearly between the two groups of candidates, it is suggested that they are presented separately:

- Presentation of candidates for baptism
- Question to candidates for baptism
- Optional testimony by candidates for baptism
- Presentation of candidates for confirmation (only)
- Question to candidates for confirmation (only)
- Optional testimony by candidates for confirmation (only)
- Question to whole congregation.

When there are many candidates, testimony may have to be omitted but the distinct identities of the two groups of candidates can still be maintained. The candidates for confirmation can wait in their seats while the candidates for baptism are presented, and then the latter can stand to one side for the presentation of the former. The two groups can then come together for the bishop's final question to the whole congregation.

Both groups of candidates make the Decision together, but only the candidates for baptism are signed with the cross. Depending on the number of candidates, it may be appropriate for the candidates for confirmation to step aside at this point, before following the candidates for baptism in the procession to the font. After the latter have been baptized (CI: p. 116), before the bishop sprinkles the congregation, the candidates for confirmation may, one at a time, approach the font, put their right hand in the water, and make the sign of the cross, either over their body or on their forehead. This can be a powerful symbolic action, not only signifying the relationship between baptism and confirmation, but also that confirmation is the candidate's response to the ongoing call of God in Christ Jesus in the life of the baptized. It also has the advantage of being visually different from baptism, which is administered by the bishop or another minister. A hymn, chant or anthem may be sung as this is happening, and continue while the bishop sprinkles the congregation. Another way of distinguishing between the two groups of candidates is to give the lighted candle to those who have just been baptized at this point in the rite rather than as part of the Sending Out. Although CW allows candles to be given to the newly confirmed as well (CI: p. 131, note 14), many of them will have already been given a candle at their baptism, and it would seem to confuse the symbolic link between baptism and enlightenment to give a candle to candidates for confirmation. If the newly baptized are not to be clothed, they may be given the candle immediately after their baptism. If clothing takes place, the candle may be given once this has been completed. If candles are given at this point, sponsors will need to hold them for the confirmation, or they will need to be put on the altar or in a pricket stand or tray of sand until the end of the rite.

Both groups of candidates are confirmed together with no distinction made between them. The Welcome is much more difficult to perform, as this only applies to the newly baptized. Those previously baptized and now confirmed are already part of the 'fellowship of faith' (CI: p. 120), and yet the congregation will naturally want to congratulate and greet both groups of candidates. Some diocesan versions of the rite get round this by omitting the Welcome altogether, and moving straight into the Peace. An alternative is to welcome the candidates for baptism earlier in the rite, after they have been given their candle. The disadvantage of this is that it separates confirmation from baptism, and so is less than ideal. Perhaps the best option is, after the liturgical welcome of the newly baptized, to introduce the applause with words similar to 'As we welcome those who have been baptized, let us also congratulate them together with those who have been confirmed'.

If the candidates are going to bring up the gifts in the offertory procession, it may be appropriate for one of the newly baptized to carry one and one of those already baptized to carry the other. The remainder of the rite continues as described above, with the Commission addressed to both groups of candidates. If Eucharistic Prayer G is used, the intercession will need to be modified to encompass both groups of candidates:

> Remember, Lord, those who have been baptized and confirmed today.
> Within the company of Christ's pilgrim people
> may *they* daily be renewed by his anointing Spirit
> until *they* come to the inheritance of your saints in glory.

Confirmation at the Eucharist

It is often the case that, when there are candidates to be confirmed who have previously been baptized, there are no candidates to be baptized at the same service. In CW certain adaptations are made to the rite for Baptism and Confirmation within Holy Communion (CI: pp. 124–5). In terms of performance, the guidance already given should be followed, and adapted as necessary.

The Liturgy of Initiation begins with the Presentation (CI: p. 111), and the candidates may be presented by their sponsors. The bishop then puts the two questions to the candidates, after which testimony may be given. After the bishop has asked the whole congregation for their welcome and support, the rite moves on to the Decision. The principal difference here is that it is not followed by the Signing with the Cross. After the last question has been put to the candidates, the bishop says the prayer at the bottom of page 113 of CI with hands outstretched, palms down, over the candidates.

The procession to the font takes place as before with water carried to the font and poured into it once people have gathered. CW provides a *berakah*-style prayer of thanksgiving (CI: p. 125) which may be said in place of the Prayer over the Water, the bishop's hands held in the *orans* position until they are brought together for Trinitarian acclamation. After the Profession of Faith, the candidates may be invited to sign themselves with the water of baptism (see p. 99) while music is sung or played, after which the bishop may sprinkle the congregation before saying the final prayer (CI: p. 117).

Given that baptism and confirmation are not being celebrated together, there may be less reason to celebrate confirmation at the font, but this is still a possibility. If not, the procession returns to the place where the Presentation and Decision took place. Confirmation is celebrated as previously described and leads into the Peace. The Welcome is omitted if there are no candidates for baptism. The newly confirmed may greet people as they walk through the church and then bring up the elements in the offertory procession. In Eucharistic Prayer G, the prayer for the candidates may be adapted, as follows:

> Remember, Lord, *N* and *N*,
> who have confirmed the promises of their baptism.
> Within the company of Christ's pilgrim people
> may *they* daily be renewed by his anointing Spirit
> until *they* come to the inheritance of your saints in glory.

The newly confirmed should receive first, even if some of them are already communicants. The Commission may follow the Prayer after

Communion and take the form on page 119 of CI, with the previously suggested change to the opening line:

> Those who are baptized and fed at the Lord's table
> are called to worship and serve God.

For reasons already given (pp. 99–100), it is suggested that the Giving of a Lighted Candle is omitted, so that the Commission leads into the Blessing and Dismissal, after which the bishop may lead the candidates through the church.

Confirmation apart from the Eucharist

The celebration of confirmation outside the Eucharist is far from ideal. In Turrell's words:

> Anglican divines argued that through participating in the eucharist one renews one's baptism. Apart from the eucharist, the confirmation rite is a little squib of a rite, cut loose from sacramental moorings, and generally unsatisfying in its shape and performance.
>
> (Turrell 2013: p. 40)

That said, if there is a particular reason why this is necessary, the order on pages 126–7 of CI is followed.

Baptism and confirmation within a Vigil Service

An exception to what has just been said may be the celebration of baptism and confirmation within a vigil service (CI: pp. 132–49). This is intended for use on the Eve of the Baptism of Christ or on Saturdays in Epiphany, on Saturdays in Eastertide, and on the Eve of All Saints' Day, or on Saturdays between All Saints and Advent Sunday. It is an episcopal service which is most likely to be celebrated when there are a significant number of candidates, either as a diocesan service in the cathedral, or as a deanery service in a large parish church. In the way it is constructed, it can only be used if there are candidates for baptism *and* confirmation. The Eucharist is not included within the rite because it is assumed that the newly baptized and confirmed will make their communion in their home parish the following morning. For guidance on the performance of a vigil service, see ALG 5 (pp. 106–7). For the celebration of Christian initiation at the Easter Vigil, see ALG 6 (pp. 80–3).

6

Rites of affirmation and reception

The journey along the Way of Christ is lifelong. A number of the Rites of Affirmation (CI: pp. 181–224) express this liturgically, meeting the needs of individuals and groups at a variety of different points along the way. Some may be used alongside discipleship courses which, like Pilgrim, provide material for use after, as well as before, initiation. Each deserves careful consideration so that it may be used, when appropriate, not only to assist the candidates in their onward journey, but also to remind the wider Christian community that they are their fellow travellers.

Celebration after an initiation service outside the parish

This material (CI: pp. 182–3) is intended for use when baptism, confirmation and/or affirmation of baptismal faith have been celebrated outside the parish church, for example in the cathedral or at another church within the deanery. Its purpose is to enable the local congregation to celebrate with the candidates, welcome them, and pray for them. This is particularly appropriate if some of the catechumenal rites have been celebrated during the candidates' preparation, and also important if, for whatever reason, the candidates have not, hitherto, been particularly visible within the worshipping life of the parish. It is intended to be used at the principal service on the Sunday following the initiation service.

The brief Pastoral Introduction may be adapted by the president for use during the Gathering. It could also be printed in that Sunday's notice sheet, together with the names of the candidates, or on a prayer card for people to take home.

The material includes a bidding for use during the intercessions, alongside a more substantial rite of Welcome which leads into the Peace. When the Welcome is used, the candidates may be invited to come forward after the intercessions and face the congregation. The president addresses two questions to the congregation, after which applause may be appropriate. The use of the second is problematic if the group includes candidates other than those who have been baptized (see p. 1). It is therefore suggested that the first line of the response is omitted, so that it reads:

> We are children of the same heavenly Father;
> we welcome you.

There is then an opportunity for testimony to be given. Whether and how this is done will depend on the number of candidates, but it may provide a useful occasion for one or more of the candidates to reflect briefly on their experience of the initiation service. The candidates then turn to face the president, who introduces the Peace. The candidates may share the peace with the whole congregation, and bring forward the elements at the offertory.

If the form of intercession provided is not used during the prayers (though the candidates should certainly be prayed for), it may be adapted for use in Eucharistic Prayer G:

> Remember, Lord, *N* and *N*.
> May they continue to grow in the grace of Christ,
> take their place among the company of your people,
> and reflect your glory in the world.

Thanksgiving for Holy Baptism

Thanksgiving for Holy Baptism (CI: pp. 184–7) may be used as the final staged rite within the catechumenal process 'some weeks after initiation' (CI: p. 184, note 1). It has been suggested that, rather than celebrating it on a Sunday, it may be more appropriately used on a weekday, perhaps at an evening Eucharist that concludes one of the Pilgrim courses (see p. 31). The problem with having the service on a weekday, however, is that it is unlikely that many of the Sunday congregation will be present, thus preventing them from responding to the Commission. That said, if the Commission was used at the candidates' baptism and/or confirmation, it could be omitted from this rite, and used at another time when the congregation is renewing its baptismal promises (CI: p. 196).

The rite is derived from the Thanksgiving for Holy Baptism (CWMV: pp. 48–9; DP: pp. 306–7) which can be inserted at the end of Morning or Evening Prayer. Although it would be possible to use this service in the same way, it would be more appropriate for it to be incorporated within the Eucharist. It is not entirely clear who this service is intended for. Note 1 refers to the 'newly initiated', whereas the rubric at the bottom of page 185 of CI also mentions those who 'have recently affirmed their baptismal faith'. There is nothing in the content of the rite that makes it inappropriate for the latter, but care needs to be taken not to refer to them as 'newly initiated'.

At the Eucharist, after the sermon, the ministers, candidates, sponsors and congregation gather at the font. During Eastertide, the Easter Candle should be carried to the font and, if possible, placed in a stand. The wording of the rubric, '*This prayer of thanksgiving is said and water may be poured into the font*', is odd. Water should be poured into the font first, perhaps by one of the candidates, and then the prayer of thanksgiving said, the president's hands being held in the *orans* position until the Trinitarian doxology. If the Commission is used, it follows now, its questions addressed to the whole congregation, not just the candidates. During the final prayer (CI: p. 185), the president's hands are held in the *orans* position.

Here there is another opportunity for testimony. On a weekday evening, this could take the form of a more informal conversation between the president and the candidates, perhaps about their experience of baptism/confirmation/affirmation, of being a communicant member of the Church, and of hopes for the future as their journey continues.

The next part of the service consists of prayers of intercession, the sprinkling of the congregation, and the Affirmation of the Christian Way (CI: p. 186). It is not obvious how these different elements relate to each other, and there is a danger that the rite can become disjointed. An alternative would be to begin with an opportunity for free prayer, either spoken or silent, leading into the Affirmation, in which the president could say the words in ordinary type, sponsors take it in turns to read the parts in italics, and the rest of the congregation respond with the words printed in bold. The sprinkling could follow (or members of the congregation could approach the font to sign themselves with the water) and lead into the Peace. After this, all may return to where the service started, someone carrying the Easter Candle, if it was brought to the font. If there is sufficient room around the altar, the congregation may be encouraged to gather in a semi-circle. The blessing on page 187 of CI would be appropriate at the conclusion of the rite.

A form for the corporate renewal of baptismal vows

With the renewed emphasis on the significance of baptism for the vocation and identity of individuals and communities (see pp. xi–xii), there is a danger that the relatively recent liturgical phenomenon of the corporate renewal of baptismal vows will be overused. The form provided (CI: pp. 193–6) is designed for use within a service *other than* baptism or confirmation and, according to the notes, 'should be used only when there has been due notice and proper preparation . . . no more than once or twice in any one year' (CI: p. 193, note 1). If one of these is the Easter Vigil (see ALG 6: pp. 80–3), another could be the feast of the Baptism of Christ, or the church's patronal or dedication festival.

It is most likely to be used at the principal Sunday Eucharist and, in this context, is inserted between the sermon and the prayers, replacing the Creed (CI: p. 193, note 2). If the congregation is to be sprinkled (CI: p. 194, note 3) the whole rite may take place at the font. After the sermon, a procession forms, and the servers and ministers process to the font. A hymn, song or chant may be sung, and the congregation turns to face the font. In Eastertide, the Easter Candle may lead the procession. At other times in the year, it may be led by acolytes and crucifer, and the Easter Candle be lit before the service, so that people can see it as they enter. Water may be carried in the procession in a jug or ewer, perhaps by an adult who has been baptized in the past year. If there are a number of servers and ministers, there is no need for them all to process, unless there is sufficient room for them to gather without obscuring the view of the congregation. Once at the font, water is poured into it, and the president may say the prayer of thanksgiving from the rite of Thanksgiving for Holy Baptism (CI: p. 184). The president then introduces the renewal of vows in his or her own words before addressing the questions from the Decision to the whole congregation. The petition that follows seems unnecessary, and can interrupt the flow of the service. After the final response, the president may introduce the Profession of Faith. At the end, the president sprinkles the congregation, preferably using a sprig of rosemary. It will normally be necessary to move among the congregation to do this, at least down and up the centre aisle or, in a larger building, along the side aisles as well, during which a chant, hymn, song or anthem may be sung. Returning to the font, the president says the prayer 'Almighty God' (CI: p. 195) with hands in the *orans* position, bringing them together at the last line.

CW allows for the Affirmation of Commitment (the Commission from the rites of baptism and confirmation) to follow (CI: p. 196). The suggestion here is that this is postponed until the Dismissal, and that the service continues with the Prayers of Intercession, led by an individual or group from the font. It would be appropriate for the prayers to include the names of all candidates for baptism, confirmation and affirmation (adults and children) in the past year, together with those participating in any discipleship courses currently running. At the end of the intercessions, the president introduces the Peace, and may share it with the congregation as the procession moves towards the altar and the offertory hymn begins.

After the Post Communion Prayer, the president may lead the Affirmation of Commitment, introducing it as follows:

> Those who are baptized and fed at the Lord's table
> are called to worship and serve God.

At the end, since the Commission is addressed to the whole congregation, the commentary's suggestion that the prayer following the Commission might lead straight into the Blessing would work well:

> May Christ dwell in your hearts through faith,
> that you may be rooted and grounded in love
> and bring forth the fruit of the Spirit,
> and the blessing . . .   (CI: p. 338)

Affirmation of Baptismal Faith

This rite, advocated by the Toronto Statement (Holeton 1993: p. 246) and *On the Way* (1995: p. 101) has no equivalent in BCP 1662 or ASB. Its presence reflects a desire to respond to varying patterns of Christian discipleship which exist today, and is intended for 'those who are already baptized and confirmed and who, after preparation and instruction, come to make a public act of commitment' (CI: p. 209, note 1). This may be a person who, at some point after she was confirmed, stopped attending church. Having re-established contact, she has been attending a discipleship course alongside candidates for baptism and confirmation, and is now ready to make a public act of commitment in which she will be reminded of the promises of her baptism and be given the opportunity to express her faith in Christ and her renewed relationship with the Church. In some church communities, if a candidate was baptized as an infant, there may be a desire for re-baptism. This is forbidden in the Church of England and throughout the Anglican Communion: 'Baptism once received is unrepeatable and any rites of renewal must avoid being misconstrued as rebaptism' (Holeton 1993: p. 229). However, responding to pressure in some parts of the Church 'for more vivid recognition of post-baptismal experiences of personal renewal and commitment', the Liturgical Commission's commentary allows for 'significant amounts of water' to be used 'without giving any appearance of a second baptism'. That the rite allows the candidates to dip themselves in the water (presumably a baptismal pool), as well as to sign themselves with the water, makes this difficult, but the commentary is clear that 'it is important to remember that however significant for the person, this is a personal reminder of the baptism that has already taken place, and that no words are used' (CI: p. 350). It is also significant that this water ritual is not administered by the president or another minister.

The rite may be celebrated at a Sunday service or as a stand-alone rite. It is also common for candidates to affirm their baptismal faith alongside candidates for baptism and/or confirmation (see pp. 112–14). Given the striking similarity between this rite and that of confirmation, it can sometimes be very difficult to distinguish between the different groups of candidates. For the purposes of this guide, consideration will first be given to Affirmation at the Sunday Eucharist and then how the rite is used when there are different groups of candidates.

Structure and content

Guidance is provided on how to order the Sunday Eucharist when it is combined with the Affirmation of Baptismal Faith (CI: p. 209, note 4). The following table gives a possible outline order.

Table 6.1 Order for the Affirmation of Baptismal Faith at the Sunday Eucharist

	Mandatory	Optional
¶ Preparation		
		Entrance Hymn
	The Greeting	
		Introduction
		Gloria in excelsis
	The Collect	
¶ The Liturgy of the Word		
		Reading(s)
		Gospel Acclamation
	Gospel reading	
	Sermon	
¶ Affirmation of Baptismal Faith		
	Presentation of the Candidates	
		The Decision
		Procession to the Font
	Profession of Faith	
	Declaration	
	(with optional signing with water or sprinkling)	
		Procession to the place of Affirmation
	Affirmation of Baptismal Faith	
		Commission
		Prayers of Intercession
		Welcome
	Peace	
¶ The Liturgy of the Eucharist		
		Offertory Hymn
	Preparation of the Table	
	Taking of the Bread and Wine	
	The Eucharistic Prayer	
	The Lord's Prayer	
	Breaking of the Bread	
	Giving of Communion	
	Prayer after Communion	
¶ The Sending Out		
		Final hymn
		Giving of a Candle
		The Blessing
	The Dismissal	

This is not an episcopal service and may be presided over by a priest (CI: p. 209, note 2), but it would nevertheless be appropriate for it to be celebrated during a bishop's visit. As with baptism and confirmation, the presentation of candidates is optional, but the questions that follow it are not (CI: p. 200). Like baptism, but unlike confirmation (there seems to be no logic to this), the candidates may be presented before the Collect or after the Sermon. The Decision is mandatory for baptism and confirmation, but optional in this rite (CI: p. 201), being used 'if pastorally desirable'. Since the renewal of baptismal promises is at the heart of this rite, it is hard to envisage a circumstance in which it would not be appropriate to include the Decision. After the Decision, there is a procession to the font, but no direction to pour water into the font or to give thanks for it. The Declaration (CI: p. 203) which, structurally, replaces baptism in the baptism rite, has no equivalent in other rites. Signing with water or sprinkling may follow the Declaration. The Affirmation itself takes place 'before the congregation' (CI: p. 203), thus leaving open the possibility of a choice of locations, as with confirmation. The Affirmation contains a strongly worded pneumatic prayer (CI: p. 204), praying that the candidates may be equipped 'with the gifts of the Holy Spirit'. A further similarity with the confirmation rite is that it is said while the 'president extends his/her hands' towards the candidates. Like confirmation, it is followed by a formula that accompanies the laying on of hands, and it concludes with the classic confirmation prayer, 'Defend, O Lord'. A further family likeness is the option to anoint the candidates (CI: p. 348). The Commission is optional and may take place after the Affirmation or at the beginning of the Sending Out. The Prayers of Intercession are also optional. Two further optional elements are mentioned in the notes but not printed in the main rite: the Welcome, which may precede the Peace, and the Giving of a Lighted Candle, which, presumably, may be included in the Sending Out (CI: p. 209, note 4). The possibility of including the Welcome is very confusing since, when baptism and confirmation are combined, it is only used for the newly baptized (CI: p. 120), and when confirmation is celebrated without baptism, it is omitted (CI: p. 125). As for the giving of the candle, it is suggested that it should only be used with candidates for baptism (see pp. 99–100).

Performance

Much of the guidance given in the previous chapter is relevant here. Candidates may be presented by sponsors, if they have them (see pp. 84–5) or, alternatively, by those involved in leading the discipleship course, or one of the ministry team. The words 'welcome *these candidates* and' are printed in squared brackets (CI: p. 200) as they may be omitted if the candidates are already well known to members of the community. This should also be borne in mind when they are presented. The following may suffice:

> Brothers and sisters, N has been journeying with us
>   along the Way of Christ.
> I present *him* to you as *he* comes to affirm *his* baptismal faith.

The Decision and procession to the font happen as at confirmation. Although there is no provision for a prayer over the water, it is suggested that water is carried in the procession and, once all have gathered, poured into the font, and that the prayer from the Thanksgiving for Holy Baptism (CI: p. 184) is used. This would be part of the rite if confirmation and affirmation were combined, and there seems to be no good reason not to include it here. The president then leads the Profession of Faith, followed by the Declaration, remaining at the font and facing the candidates to introduce it. The candidates then face the congregation to declare their faith (as a group rather than individually). The signing with water and sprinkling also mirror the confirmation rite.

A decision has to be made about whether the Affirmation takes place at the font or where the rite began. The suggestion here is that it should happen at the font. This enables an obvious connection to be made between the affirmation of baptismal faith and the place of baptism. Standing in an arc in front of the president, the president extends his or her hands over the candidates and says the first prayer on page 204 of CI. As with confirmation, although it is made clear that the oil of chrism can be used, no guidance is given as to when and how (see pp. 91–2). It is recommended that the same method is employed in both rites. However, if it is desired to highlight a distinction between the two, the Toronto Statement suggests that candidates for affirmation be invited to sign themselves with chrism before the laying on of hands (Holeton 1993: p. 247). (For more detailed discussion, see ALG 4: pp. 48–9.)

After the last candidate has received the anointing and the laying on of hands, the congregation prays the confirmation prayer (CI: p. 204). The Prayers of Intercession are optional, and it is suggested that they are omitted, and that the service leads into the Peace. The candidates can then share the peace among the congregation before returning to the font and following the procession back to the altar, carrying the bread and wine for the Eucharist.

If Eucharistic Prayer G is used, the following intercession may be included:

> Remember, Lord, *N* and *N*.
> May they continue to grow in the grace of Christ,
> take their place among the company of your people,
> and reflect your glory in the world.

At Holy Communion the candidates may receive first, as a group, or with their family and friends. The Commission may be used after the Post Communion Prayer, the candidates standing in front of the president as at the Presentation. After the Blessing and Dismissal, the president may lead them through the congregation.

Affirmation of Baptismal Faith apart from the Eucharist

This guide encourages the Affirmation to take place within the context of the Eucharist. When, for whatever reason, it is combined with a Service of the Word or Morning or Evening Prayer, notes 5 and 6 (CI: p. 210) provide guidance on how the rite should be ordered.

Affirmation of Baptismal Faith at a celebration of Baptism and/or Confirmation

Members of a discipleship course will sometimes include those who are already baptized and confirmed as well as those who wish to prepare for Christian initiation. CW permits baptism, confirmation and affirmation to be celebrated together. While this has the strong advantage of enabling the group to work together towards the same liturgical staging-post (albeit involving participation in different rites), the difficulty this presents is maintaining a distinction between the groups of candidates.

The rite of Baptism and Confirmation within a Celebration of Holy Communion (CI: pp. 108–23) provides guidance on how affirmation should be incorporated. In terms of performance, the following points should be borne in mind. For simplicity, the principal distinction needs to be drawn between one group containing candidates for baptism *and* confirmation, and another with candidates for confirmation (only) and affirmation. Thus, at the Presentation, in order to distinguish between these two groups, the candidates may be presented in the following order:

- Presentation of candidates for baptism
- Question to candidates for baptism
- Optional testimony by candidates for baptism
- Presentation of candidates for confirmation (only) and affirmation
- Questions to candidates for confirmation (only) and affirmation
- Optional testimony by candidates for confirmation (only) and affirmation
- Question to whole congregation.

The candidates for affirmation can wait in their seats with the confirmands while the candidates for baptism are presented, and then the latter can stand to one side for the presentation of the candidates for confirmation and affirmation. The two groups come together for the bishop's final question to the whole congregation.

As the rite continues the candidates for affirmation and confirmation (only) participate in the same way until they sign themselves with water from the font (CI: p. 117). At that point, after the baptisms have taken place (and the newly baptized have been clothed and/or received their candles, if this takes place at the font), the newly baptized and the candidates for confirmation (only) step to one side, allowing the affirmands to stand in front of the president for the Declaration (CI: p. 203). After they have declared their faith, they approach the font to sign themselves, followed by the candidates for confirmation (only), before the bishop sprinkles the whole congregation.

The Affirmation follows the Confirmation (CI: p. 118). Whether it takes place at the font or at the front of the church, the candidates for affirmation stand to one side while the newly baptized and the confirmands are confirmed. After the last person has been confirmed, these candidates move to the side while the affirmands stand or kneel in their place and the bishop says the prayer over them. After the anointing and laying on of hands, all the candidates come together in one group and face the people as they pray for them (CI: p. 119).

If the Welcome is used for the newly baptized (CI: p. 120), the bishop may say afterwards: 'As we welcome those who have been baptized, let us also congratulate them together with those who have been confirmed and those who have affirmed their faith in Christ', and the congregation may applaud all the candidates before the bishop introduces the Peace.

Reception into the communion of the Church of England

Canon B28 governs reception into the Church of England. The rite provided is intended for those who have been 'episcopally confirmed with unction or with the laying on of hands' (Canon B28.3) who may be received, with the permission of the bishop, after they have received instruction. The commentary notes that the interpretation of this requirement

> has become more complex in the light of increased use of presbyteral confirmation (with episcopally consecrated chrism) in the Roman Catholic Church, the regular practice of presbyteral confirmation (without chrism) in the Nordic and Baltic churches of the Porvoo Agreement, and continuing debate about how presbyteral chrismation is to be understood in the Eastern churches. (CI: p. 350)

In 2009 the Legal Advisory Commission was asked to give an opinion on Canon B28, and concluded that 'Presbyteral confirmation in the Roman Catholic Church and chrismation within the Orthodox Churches are both forms of episcopal confirmation within the meaning of Canon B28, paragraph 3' (Legal Advisory Commission of the General Synod, *Ordinands: Requirement of Confirmation*, 2009). If there is still any doubt in the mind of the parish priest as to how a person from another Christian denomination should be received, the advice of the bishop or diocesan registrar should be sought. (For a more detailed discussion of this issue, see Christopher Hill, 'The Minister of Confirmation' in Avis 2011: pp. 101–5.)

More straightforwardly, those who have not been baptized, or the validity of whose baptism is in doubt, are received when they are baptized or conditionally baptized (Canon B28.1). Finally, those who have been baptized but not episcopally confirmed are received through confirmation (Canon B28.2).

Candidates who are received using the CW rite (CI: pp. 211–22) may include those who, having had little contact with their previous church community for some time, have been part of a discipleship course, as well as those who, having been active members of another denomination, have requested to be received into the communion of the Church of England. In responding liturgically to any request, pastoral sensitivity is required so that the candidate's journey thus far is not, in any way, belittled or overlooked. Except in the case of the reception of a priest, the president of the rite may be the parish priest. When a priest is received, a bishop or the bishop's commissary must preside (Canon B28.3).

Reception at a weekday Eucharist

The way that CW presents the rite suggests a high-profile public service. Although it is framed within the same structure as the rites of initiation and the affirmation of baptismal faith, in many cases it may be more appropriate for reception to be a more low-key affair, perhaps incorporated into a weekday Eucharist, attended by close family and friends. It is also more likely to be the case that there is one candidate at any one time, rather than several.

After the sermon, the president asks the candidate if she has been baptized and is now ready to affirm her faith in Jesus Christ (CI: p. 214). Although the Decision may follow (CI: p. 215), it is only really appropriate if the candidate considers reception to be an opportunity to renew her baptismal promises. If not, the rite continues with the Profession of Faith (CI: p. 216), said by the whole congregation. CW directs that the ministers and candidates gather at the font for this, but at a weekday celebration this may not be necessary, unless the rite is viewed as including the renewal of baptismal promises. The Declaration follows (CI: p. 217), the candidate facing the president to answer the questions. If this takes place at the font, the candidate may then sign herself with water, and the president may sprinkle the congregation before saying the concluding prayer, hands held in the *orans* position. If there has been no procession to the font, the prayer of reception follows (CI: p. 218), for which the candidate may remain standing. If the congregation has gathered at the font, the reception may take place here. The president, with hands extended over the candidate, says the prayer (CI: p. 218). Then, taking the candidate's right hand (as if they are shaking hands), the president says the formula of reception before inviting the congregation to respond with the confirmation prayer. The commentary suggests that the oil of chrism may be used as part of the rite (CI: p. 348), but it is not at all clear when this might be done and how; nor is it considered appropriate to incorporate the Welcome or Giving of a Lighted Candle (CI: p. 223, note 4). If appropriate, the Commission may be used after reception or at the end of the rite.

If a candidate is received at a Service of the Word, or at Morning or Evening Prayer, guidance is provided in notes 5 and 6 (CI: p. 224).

Reception before Affirmation of Baptismal Faith

In some cases, if a (baptized and confirmed) Christian has had no regular contact with their previous denomination for some time, and is now a member of a discipleship course, it may be appropriate for them to prepare with other candidates for a public affirmation of baptismal faith, and for them to be received as part of their preparation for that. This could happen as part of the worship before or after one of the sessions, or at a weekday service. Since a public affirmation of faith is to follow, the reception could be reduced to the Declaration (CI: p. 217) and the formula for reception (CI: p. 218), followed by appropriate prayers for the candidate and other members of the group. In such a case, it would be appropriate to seek the bishop's support before receiving a candidate in this way.

Reception into the communion of the Church of England at a celebration of Baptism and/or Confirmation and/or Affirmation of Baptismal Faith

When a person is received at a service in which other candidates are baptized and/or confirmed and/or affirm their baptismal faith, most of the principles outlined above apply (see pp. 112–14), not least the importance of distinguishing candidates for reception from those for initiation or affirmation. Once again, the rite of Baptism and Confirmation within a Celebration of Holy Communion is used (CI: pp. 108–23). Its rubrics note where elements from the reception rite are to be inserted. In this case, unless the particular circumstances of the candidate suggests otherwise, he or she should be presented separately from the others. If the rite contains candidates for baptism and confirmation, confirmation (only), affirmation and reception, the presentation could follow this sequence (as the number of categories increases, so should the likelihood that any testimony will be given in written form rather than orally):

- Presentation of candidates for baptism
- Question to candidates for baptism
- Optional testimony by candidates for baptism
- Presentation of candidates for confirmation (only) and affirmation
- Questions to candidates for confirmation (only) and affirmation
- Optional testimony by candidates for confirmation (only) and affirmation
- Presentation of candidates for reception
- Questions to candidates for reception
- Optional testimony by candidates for reception
- Question to whole congregation.

In this rite, the Decision is not optional for those to be received (CI: p. 112), but they are not signed with the cross. The Declaration (CI: p. 217) is inserted after candidates for affirmation, if any, have made their Declaration, after which candidates for reception may be invited to sign themselves with water, along with the confirmands and affirmands. The reception itself (CI: p. 218) follows the rite of affirmation or, if there are no candidates for this, it follows confirmation. Those to be received stand to one side during the rites of confirmation and affirmation. After the last affirmand has received the anointing and hand-laying, these candidates move to the side while those to be received stand in their place and the bishop says the prayer over them. After the bishop has received them, all the candidates come together in one group and face the people as they pray for them (CI: p. 119).

At the Welcome (CI: p. 120), if the liturgical welcome is used for the newly baptized (CI: p. 120), the bishop may afterwards encourage applause by saying: 'As we welcome those who have been baptized, let us also congratulate them together with those who have been confirmed, those who have affirmed their faith in Christ, and those who have been received into the communion of the Church of England.'

Sources and further reading

Liturgical texts

The Book of Common Prayer, The Church of England (1662).

The Book of Common Prayer, The Episcopal Church (New York: The Church Hymnal Corporation, 1979).

The Book of Occasional Services 2003, The Episcopal Church (New York: The Church Hymnal Corporation, 2004).

Church of England Liturgical Commission, *Rules to Order the Service and Other Miscellaneous Liturgical Proposals* (London: General Synod of the Church of England, 1342, 1999).

Common Worship: Christian Initiation (London: Church House Publishing, 2006).

Common Worship: Christian Initiation. Additional Baptism Texts in Accessible Language (London: Church House Publishing, 2015).

Common Worship: Ordination Services (London: Church House Publishing, 2007).

Common Worship: A Pastoral Ministry Companion (London: Church House Publishing, 2012).

Common Worship: Daily Prayer (London: Church House Publishing, 2005).

Common Worship: Pastoral Services (2nd edn, London: Church House Publishing, 2005).

Common Worship: Services and Prayers for the Church of England (London: Church House Publishing, 2000).

Common Worship: Times and Seasons (London: Church House Publishing, 2006).

New Patterns for Worship (London: Church House Publishing, 2002).

Rite of Baptism for Children, Roman Catholic Church (London: Geoffrey Chapman, 1993).

Rite of Christian Initiation of Adults, Roman Catholic Church (London: Geoffrey Chapman, 1987).

Studies, guides and other works

Avis, Paul (ed.), *The Journey of Christian Initiation* (London: Church House Publishing, 2011).

Bradshaw, Paul (ed.), *A Companion to Common Worship Volume 1*, Alcuin Club Collection 78 (London: SPCK, 2001).

Bradshaw, Paul (ed.), *A Companion to Common Worship Volume 2*, Alcuin Club Collection 81 (London: SPCK, 2006).

Bradshaw, Paul and Johnson, Maxwell, *The Origins of Feasts, Fasts and Seasons in Early Christianity*, Alcuin Club Collections 86 (London: SPCK, 2011).

Brind, Jan and Wilkinson, Tessa, *Creative Ideas for Pastoral Liturgy: Baptism, Confirmation and Liturgies for the Journey* (Norwich: Canterbury Press, 2010).

Buchanan, Colin, *Baptism as Complete Sacramental Initiation*, Grove Worship Series 219 (Cambridge: Grove Books, 2014).

The Ceremonial of Bishops (Collegeville, MN: Liturgical Press, 1989).

Croft, Steven, et al., *Pilgrim: Leader's Guide* (London: Church House Publishing, 2013).

Dalby, Mark, *Admission to Communion: The Approaches of the Late Medievals and the Reformers*, Joint Liturgical Study 75 (Norwich: Hymns A&M, 2013).

Dalby, Mark, *Infant Communion: The New Testament to the Reformation*, Joint Liturgical Study 56 (Cambridge: Grove Books, 2003).

Dalby, Mark, *Infant Communion: Post-Reformation to Present Day*, Joint Liturgical Study 67 (Norwich: Hymns A&M, 2009).

Dearmer, Percy, *The Parson's Handbook*, 12th edn (London: Oxford University Press, 1932).

A Directory of Ceremonial, Part I, Alcuin Club Tracts XIII, 2nd edn (London: Mowbray, 1947).

Earey, Mark, Lloyd, Trevor and Tarrant, Ian, *Connecting with Baptism* (London: Church House Publishing, 2007).

Elliott, Peter, *Ceremonies of the Liturgical Year According to the Modern Roman Rite* (San Francisco, CA: Ignatius Press, 2002).

Elliott, Peter, *Ceremonies of the Modern Roman Rite* (San Francisco, CA: Ignatius Press, 1995).

The English Ritual, new edn (Norwich: Canterbury Press, 2002).

Giles, Richard, *Creating Uncommon Worship* (Norwich: Canterbury Press, 2004).

Giles, Richard, *Re-Pitching the Tent* (Norwich: Canterbury Press, 1997).

Giles, Richard, *Times and Seasons* (Norwich: Canterbury Press, 2008).

Gordon-Taylor, Benjamin and Jones, Simon, *Celebrating Christ's Appearing*, Alcuin Liturgy Guides 5 (London: Alcuin Club/SPCK, 2008).

Gordon-Taylor, Benjamin and Jones, Simon, *Celebrating Christ's Victory*, Alcuin Liturgy Guides 6 (London: Alcuin Club/SPCK, 2009).

Gordon-Taylor, Benjamin and Jones, Simon, *Celebrating the Eucharist*, Alcuin Liturgy Guides 3 (London: Alcuin Club/SPCK, 2005 and 2011).

Haselock, Jeremy, 'Introduction', in Myers, Gilly, *Using Common Worship: Initiation Services* (London: Church House Publishing/Praxis, 2000), pp. 1–20.

Holeton, David (ed.), *Growing in Newness of Life: Christian Initiation in Anglicanism Today* (Toronto: Anglican Book Centre, 1993).

Irvine, Christopher (ed.), *The Use of Symbols in Worship*, Alcuin Liturgy Guides 4 (London: Alcuin Club/SPCK, 2007).

Johnson, Maxwell, *The Rites of Christian Initiation*, new edn (Collegeville, MN: Pueblo/Liturgical Press, 2007).

Jones, Simon, 'Integration of Separation? The Future of Confirmation within the Church of England', *Theology* 98 (1995), pp. 282–9.

Jones, Simon, '"Outward Ceremony and Honourable Badge": The Theological Significance of the Sign of the Cross in the Baptismal Liturgies of the Church of England and Scottish Episcopal Church', in Ross, Melanie and Jones, Simon (eds), *The Serious Business of Worship* (London: T&T Clark, 2010), pp. 143–58.

Kavanagh, Aidan, *Elements of Rite* (Collegeville, MN: Pueblo, 1982).

Kuehn, Regina, *A Place for Baptism* (Chicago, IL: Liturgy Training Publications, 1992).

The Lambeth Conference 1968: Resolutions and Reports (London: SPCK, 1968).

McGrail, Peter, *The Rite of Christian Initiation: Adult Rituals and Roman Catholic Ecclesiology* (Farnham: Ashgate, 2013).

Meyers, Ruth, *Continuing the Reformation: Re-Visioning Baptism in the Episcopal Church* (New York: Church Publishing Inc., 1997).

Michno, Dennis, *A Priest's Handbook: The Ceremonies of the Church*, 3rd edn (New York: Morehouse, 1998).

Nash, Paul, *Supporting Dying Children and their Families: A Handbook for Christian Ministry* (London: SPCK, 2011).

Oliver, Stephen (ed.), *Pastoral Prayers* (London: Mowbray, 1996).

On the Way: Towards an Integrated Approach to Christian Initiation, GS Misc 444 (London: Church House Publishing, 1995).

One Baptism: Towards Mutual Recognition. A Study Text, Faith and Order Paper 210 (Geneva: World Council of Churches, 2011).

Ritual Notes (London: W. Knott & Son, 1946, 1947 and 1956).

Spinks, Bryan, *Reformation and Modern Rituals and Theologies of Baptism* (Aldershot: Ashgate, 2006).

Turner, Paul, *Celebrating Initiation: A Guide for Priests* (Franklin Park, IL: World Library Publications, 2007).

Turrell, James, *Celebrating the Rites of Initiation* (New York: Church Publishing Inc., 2013).

Ward, Tess, *Alternative Pastoral Prayers* (Norwich: Canterbury Press, 2012).

Whitehead, Nick and Whitehead, Hazel, *Baptism Matters* (London: National Society/Church House Publishing, 1998).

World Council of Churches, *Baptism, Eucharist, Ministry* (Geneva: World Council of Churches, 1982).

Yarnold, Edward, *The Awe-Inspiring Rites of Initiation* (Edinburgh: T&T Clark, 1994).

Yarnold, Edward, 'Initiation: Sacrament and Experience', in Stevenson, Kenneth (ed.), *Liturgy Reshaped* (London: SPCK, 1982), pp. 17–31.

Index

Page numbers in *italics* indicate a table of information.

adherence (*syntaxis*) 52
Admission of the Baptized to
    Communion 24–6
adult initiation
    anointing 38–9, 77, 86–7, 91–3
    Apostles' Creed 82
    Blessing 82
    celebration of initiation outside
        parish 103–4
    Collect 83
    Commission 82, 93, 94–5, 101–2
    Decision 85–6, 101
    Dismissal 96
    Giving of a Lighted Candle 82, 95–6,
        99–100, 102
    liturgy 80–2
    Liturgy of Baptism 88–90
    Liturgy of the Eucharist 94
    Liturgy of the Word 83–4
    Order for *80–1*
    Peace 93, 101
    Prayer over the Water 88, 101
    Preparation 82–3
    Presentation of the Candidates 81,
        84–5, 98–9, 101
    Profession of Faith 82, 88, 101
    Sending Out 94–6
    setting 77–80, 90–1
    Signing with the Cross 81–2, 86–7
    in vigil services 102
    Welcome 93, 100, 101, 103–4
Affirmation, rites of 35–6, 103, 107–14
affusion 61, 89
Agnus Dei 74
albs 12, 89
all-age worship 24, 25, 64–5, 71
altar 3, 5, 8–9
alternative texts (ATAL) 51–2, 53–4,
    63–4, 73, 82
ambo 7–8

anointing 16, 24
    adult initiation 38–9, 77, 86–7, 91–3
    infant baptism 44–5, 55–6, 61–2, 73
Apostles' Creed 28, 30, 40–1, 59, 82,
    88
ATAL *see* alternative texts (ATAL)
authorized services 14

balsam 44
baptism
    high demands on parents and
        godparents 15
    methods of for older children 62
    mixed age 96–7
    refusal of 15
    of those near death 76
'Baptism Buddies' 48, 54, 65–6, 67
Baptism of Candidates
    adult initiation 88–90
    infant baptism 60–3
Baptism of Christ 106
Baptismal Faith, affirmation
    at Baptism and Confirmation
        112–14
    liturgy 107–10
    Order for *109*
    setting 111–12
baptismal pools 6, 78
baptismal vows, renewal, corporate
    liturgy 106–7
Beatitudes 29
biblical readings 17, 50, 71–2, 83, 96
bishops
    role in initiation services 9–10, 78–9,
        83–4, 88
    vestments 11–13
Blessing
    adult initiation 82
    infant baptism 65–6, 75
blessing of a child 19–20

Call and Celebration of the Decision
to be Baptized or Confirmed
or to Affirm Baptismal Faith
36–9
candles 24, 43, 73
see also Easter Candle; Giving of
a Lighted Candle
certificates 21, 26, 66, 75
chairs, president's 8
chaplains 84
chrism
use in affirmation rites 111, 116
use in confirmation 91–2
use in infant baptism 43–4, 61–2,
97–8
Chrism Eucharist 44
chrismation 92–3, 114
Church members, rites for 21–2, 23
Collect
adult initiation 83
infant baptism 49–50
commended services 14
Commission
adult initiation 82, 93, 94–5,
101–2
infant baptism 63–4, 73
commitment, public act of 108
*Common Worship: Christian Initiation:
Additional Baptism Texts in
Accessible Language see* alternative
texts (ATAL)
communion
admission of the baptized 24–6
infant 69–70, 74
numbers of communicants 79–80
reception into 114–17
confirmation
after baptism 78, 91
liturgy 91–3, 98–100, 101
setting 78–80, 90–1
congregational participation 59, 89–90,
103, 104, 106–7
cottas 12
croziers 11–13, 84
Cyril, Saint, of Jerusalem 1–2, 52

dalmatics 12
deacons 10

Decision
adult initiation 85–6, 101
affirmation of baptismal faith 110
infant baptism 52–4
Declaration, affirmation of baptismal
faith 110, 111, 113
discipleship courses 103, 108
see also Pilgrim course
Dismissal
adult initiation 96
infant baptism 65–6, 75
divine initiative 52

Easter Candle 6–7
adult initiation 86, 95–6, 106
infant baptism 43, 65
Easter Liturgy 7
Easter Vigil 6–7, 106
Emergency Baptism 75–6
Eucharistic Prayers 25–6, 35, 39, 74, 94
evangelism through initiation rites 79
eye contact 85–6, 88

first communion 24–6
fixtures and fittings, ecclesiastical 3–9
font 3–6, 8, 16, 57, 101, 111
adult initiation 78
infant baptism 42–3
funerals 5

Giles, Richard 4, 5, 6
Giving of a Lighted Candle
adult initiation 82, 95–6, 99–100, 102
affirmation of baptismal faith 110
infant baptism 65–6, 75
Gloria in excelsis 83
godparents 18, 59
Gospel, as gift during initiation 17, 20, 39

homilies 17
see also sermons
hymns 16, 17

immersion 6
adults 77, 89
infants 42, 62
vestments 13
incense 7, 35

Index

infant baptism
  anointing 44–5, 55–6, 61–2, 73
  Blessing 65–6, 75
  Collect 49–50
  Commission 63–4, 73
  Decision 52–4
  Dismissal 65–6, 75
  emergency 75–6
  Giving of a Lighted Candle 65–6, 75
  liturgy 46–8
  Liturgy of Baptism 51–66, 72–4
  Liturgy of the Word 50–1, 71–2
  Order for 47, 68–9
  Peace 64–5, 73
  Prayer over the Water 57–8
  Preparation 48–50, 71
  Presentation of the Candidates 51–2
  private worship 46–8
  Profession of Faith 58–60
  public worship 66–71
  readers 50
  Sending Out 65–6
  setting 42–6, 47–8, 66–71, 72–3
  Signing with the Cross 44, 55–6
  Welcome 48–50, 64–5, 73
intercessions see Prayers of Intercession

Jesus' Summary of the Law 29
John Chrysostom, Saint 52

Kavanagh, Aidan 4–5
Kuehn, Regina 4

lay ministers 10
laying on of hands 24
  see also anointing
lectern 7–8
liturgical colours 11
liturgy
  accessibility 67
  adaptions 18, 19, 20, 22, 32, 35, 58,
    63–4, 73
  dramatic flow of 53–4, 55
  private 16–21, 46–8
  public 21–2, 106–7
Liturgy of Baptism
  adult initiation 88–90
  infant baptism 51–66, 72–4

Liturgy of Initiation
  adult initiation 84–93
  confidence in 1–2
Liturgy of the Eucharist 74, 94
Liturgy of the Word 7–8
  adult initiation 83–4
  infant baptism 50–1, 71–2
Lord's Prayer 21, 28, 30, 40–1

mitres 11–13, 84
music, use of 16, 17

naming of a child 60, 76

oil 24, 38–9, 43–5, 55–6, 76, 77, 92–3
  see also chrism

Paschal Candle see Easter Candle
pastoral opportunities 14
Peace
  adult initiation 93, 101
  infant baptism 64–5, 73
perfume 44
Pilgrim course 27, 30
Prayer over the Water
  adult initiation 88, 101
  infant baptism 57–8
Prayers of Intercession 64, 73
Preparation
  adult initiation 82–3
  infant baptism 48–50, 71
Presentation of the Candidates
  adult initiation 81, 84–5, 98–9, 101
  affirmation of baptismal faith 113
  infant baptism 51–2
  reception into the communion 117
Presentation of the Four Texts 28–9, 40–1
presidents (of the rite) 9–10
prevenient grace 51, 55, 85
private worship
  infant baptism 46–8
  Thanksgiving for the Gift of a Child
    16–21
processions 57, 72, 82, 87, 90, 96, 101,
  106
Profession of Faith
  adult initiation 82, 88, 101
  infant baptism 58–60

public worship
  Admission of the Baptized to
    Communion 24–6
  infant baptism 66–71
  Rites on the Way (adults) 33–5
  Thanksgiving for the Gift of a Child
    24–6

readers 17, 50, 83
readings 17, 50, 71–2, 83, 96
rebaptism 108
Reception into the Communion 114–17
registers 21, 26, 38
rehearsals 46, 79
renunciation (*apotaxis*) 52
rites, integration of 22, 23, 69–70
Rites on the Way (adults)
  in the Christian Year 29–30, *31*
  liturgy 28–9
  local considerations 30–2
robing the newly baptized 12, 62, 89–90

Satan 53
Sending Out 74–5
  adult initiation 94–6
  infant baptism 65–6
sermons 17, 44–5, 50–1, 72, 84
service sheets 45–6, 67–8, 78–9
setting 2–13
  adult initiation 77–80, 90–1
  infant baptism 42–6, 47–8, 66–71,
    72–3
Signing with the Cross
  adult initiation 81–2, 86–7
  infant baptism 44, 55–6
sponsors 18, 31, 34, 37, 39, 79, 84, 88
sprinkling of congregation 89, 101

stoles 12
Sunday Eucharist
  adult initiation within 97–8
  confirmation within 100–2
  infant baptism within 66–75
surplices 12
symbolic actions 43, 44–5, 54, 86,
    99–100

testimony 36, 79, 85, 96, 104, 105, 117
Thanksgiving for Baptism, liturgy 104–6
Thanksgiving for the Gift of a Child
  outside Church 22
  private liturgy 16–21
  public liturgy 21–2
  purpose 14–16
Turner, Paul 13, 89
Turrell, James 2, 36, 43, 62, 70, 74,
    85–6, 87–8, 92, 102

vestments 11–13
vigil services 102

water
  use in affirmation rites 108, 111
  use in baptismal rites 42–3, 56–8, 61,
    76, 87–8, 89–90
Welcome
  adult initiation 93, 100, 101, 103–4
  affirmation of baptismal faith 114
  infant baptism 48–50, 64–5, 73
Welcome of Disciples on the Way of
    Faith 32–5
Welcome of those Preparing for the
    Baptism of Children 23

Yarnold, Edward 1